RIVERS OF RIGHTEOUSNESS
Quiet, Quicken & Quench Your Thirst

DR. RAYMOND M. GORDON, SR.

ISBN 0-7414-4397-X

Published by:

PUBLISHING.COM

1094 New DeHaven Street, Suite 100
West Conshohocken, PA 19428-2713
Info@buybooksontheweb.com
www.buybooksontheweb.com
Toll-free (877) BUY BOOK
Local Phone (610) 941-9999
Fax (610) 941-9959

Printed in the United States of America

Printed on Recycled Paper

Published October 2007

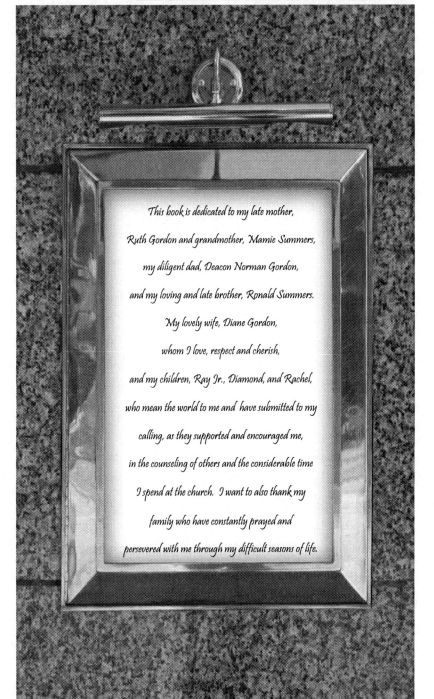

This book is dedicated to my late mother,

Ruth Gordon and grandmother, Mamie Summers,

my diligent dad, Deacon Norman Gordon,

and my loving and late brother, Ronald Summers.

My lovely wife, Diane Gordon,

whom I love, respect and cherish,

and my children, Ray Jr., Diamond, and Rachel,

who mean the world to me and have submitted to my

calling, as they supported and encouraged me,

in the counseling of others and the considerable time

I spend at the church. I want to also thank my

family who have constantly prayed and

persevered with me through my difficult seasons of life.

FOREWORD

For those seeking a compact and concise compendium of Christian faith and practice, this book by Dr. Raymond Gordon is a must. Dr. Gordon has spent many years ministering to God's people and has hungered and thirsted after God himself. It is the intense pilgrimage of searching for the deep truths of the biblical revelation, and the faithful imparting of this knowledge to faithful and equally hungering students, that this valuable work has evolved.

The reality of God and the saga of His work on behalf of fallen man is itself an awe inspiring story. The effort on the part of the believer to walk in the "newness" of life is an ever present challenge.

This book beckons the lost to "seek ye the Lord while He may be found." And it encourages the believer to "stand fast in the liberty wherewith Christ has made us free." This is certainly a valuable addition to anyone's library.

Dr. Charles Walker
Pastor
19th Street Baptist Church
Philadelphia, PA

FOREWORD

It has been my privilege to observe the life and ministry of Dr. Raymond M. Gordon, Sr., over the past two decades. This servant of God has sought to glorify his Savior and Lord Jesus Christ in dealings with his family, church, and community.

God has taken this humble pastor-teacher and has gifted him with vision for the future, compassion for souls, and a heart for the global community. In all things, Jesus Christ has been preeminent.

On several occasions I have discussed with Pastor Gordon his views on why God has so richly blessed his ministry with St. Matthew's Baptist Church. He always, first of all, reiterates the emphasis that he places on the faithful teaching of God's Word as being the primary key to the marvelous growth and expansion of the church. Then, secondly, he shares that God has blessed his church with wonderful people who have a great desire to do the work of our Lord.

God's heralds are always given the right of way in every generation. So this is true with Dr. Gordon's proclamation of God's Holy Word, the Bible. This compilation of his messages is a treasure chest of his insights into the Bible. It gives a taste of the spiritual feast that is regularly served by God's messenger at St. Matthew's Baptist Church. By desiring the sincere milk of the Word, this Pastor and this Church will continue to grow for years to come.

W. Sherrill Babb, Ph.D.
President
Philadelphia Biblical University

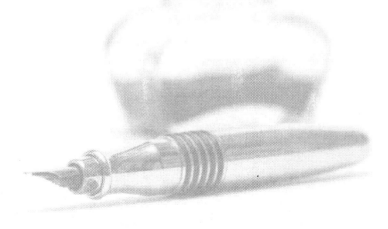

FOREWORD

Dr. Raymond Gordon, Sr. -

Has rapidly become one of the most creative, influential, charismatic and productive leaders of this generation.

In the Philadelphia area, as well as our National Baptist Convention, U.S.A., Inc. family, Dr. Gordon has risen to iconic stature.

Dr. Gordon is a classic expositor and a creative builder on an ever-expanding campus on the St. Matthew's acreage.

One soon discovers that the Raymond Gordon touch on any pursuit will soon be saturated with that incomparable presence and penetration of the One to whom He gives ALL joy: "*JESUS*."

In his preaching, speaking and now in his writing, we will always be directed to *JESUS*.

I love to hear him say, and you will love to sense him saying even in his writings: "*IT'S JESUS*."

Dr. A. Louis Patterson, Jr.
Lecturer: Ministers Division
National Baptist Congress, U.S.A., Inc.
Pastor, Mount Corinth Baptist Church
Houston, Texas

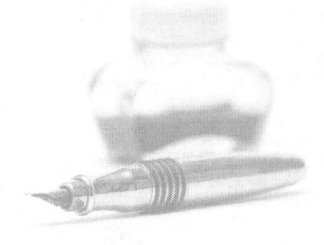

TABLE OF CONTENTS

TABLE OF CONTENTS

TABLE OF CONTENTS

TABLE OF CONTENTS

ACKNOWLEDGEMENTS

First and foremost, I must acknowledge the Lord Jesus Christ, who enabled, equipped and elected me for this ministry. Secondly, my staff, Jennifer Jennings, Kathleen Medley, Lorna Darby and Pastor Darrell Freeman, who helped to compile and prepare the book, as well as my editor, Barbara Arnold. Last but certainly not least are my personal mentors: Dr. Charles Walker, my Pastor, Dr. W. Sherrill Babb, President of Philahelphia Biblical University, and Dr. A.L. Patterson, Jr., profound expositor and friend.

INTRODUCTION

Reflection is a powerful tool of recollection. As life continues to move on, we tend to identify meaningful oasis in our lives, which counter discouragement, discontentment and dismay. Paul, the Apostle, wrote in Ephesians chapter 2 that we were Dead, Depraved, Disobedient and Doomed, but God who is rich in mercy called us out of darkness and translated us into His marvelous light. This book depicts God's calling and election of one who was doomed. God called me from the Hood to Heaven, from confusion to correction and from the system of the world to His wisdom.

Every page of this book is etched out of a pain that led to a promotion of peace. Looking back over my life, the first seventeen years was growing up in South Philadelphia, the hood. After graduation of high school, the next seven years was spent in the military branch of the Air Force doing top secret work. This was followed by five years of confusion. It was during this time of confusion that I accepted the Lord Jesus Christ as my Savior and began a journey of enlightenment, enrichment and enablement through the power of the Holy Spirit. He empowered me to attend Philadelphia Biblical University, while working. The Holy Spirit continued to endow me with His Presence and keeping Power, throughout my seventeen years of working in the U.S. Government, and then He called me to the Pastorate in 1987.

This book should serve as a Devotional tool to encourage its' readers, a Directional device to enlighten its participants, and finally, as a Discipling mechanism to lead the reader into a rich fellowship with the Lord Jesus Christ. May the pages of this book flow in your hearts as a River of Righteousness that brings about a Rest and a Reassurance of the Redemptive Power of Jesus Christ.

Dr. Raymond M. Gordon, Sr.
Senior Pastor
St. Matthew's Baptist Church
Williamstown, NJ

GOD'S MAJESTY

Bless the LORD, O my soul, O LORD my God, thou art very great; thou art clothed with honour and majesty.

Psalm 104:1

Undiminished Power

Every part of the creation of God has received a small percentage of glory and power from God. That percentage of glory emerges as that particular creation functions the way God intended for it to function. Birds were given the power of flight and the glory of aerial beauty in the midst of God's firmament. Ants were given the power to carry one hundred times their weight, and the glory of organization. Man was given the power of headship over God's earthly creation, and the glory to reflect God's communicable attributes. However, not all power and glory has been used to exalt God. The Bible talks about the power of evil, and the power of the tongue. These are nothing more than power surges, shortages of evil, and blown fuses of deception. They can only disrupt for so long, before the master power source will short circuit. One of the incommunicable attributes of God is that He has all power in His hands. He is omnipotent, meaning that God's power is infinite, that is, it is to an unknown, unimaginable, immeasurable degree. God doesn't have a percentage of power, nor was His power ever diminished. He has all power (dunamis). He has the power of thought, the extended power of His Word. *God maintains power that only He, as God, possesses.*

In our text, David makes a great preparation for the future of the house of the Lord. He is exhorting the people to give unselfishly and sacrificially, so that gold and silver will be available when Solomon is ready to build. However, in the midst of their giving, David takes time to praise God. Notice how David describes God in I Chron. 29:10-13. David reminds us that God is all-powerful. Biblically, we, as Christians can attest to at least five ways in which God is all-powerful (Omnipotent).

1. **God Possesses the Power to Create**: Because God has the power to create, *He planned His creation, He had a purpose for His creation and He provided for His creation.* Job 38:7 lets us know that the morning stars and all of the sons of God sang together and shouted for joy at Creation. It was that awesome.

2. **God Possesses the Power to Cancel**: God has all power to cancel our sin, for the Word says in Romans chapter 6, "where sin abounds, grace super abounds." God cancels our sin because He is our Redeemer. God can also cancel spiritual sickness,

as He did with the demon possessed man who called himself Legion. On the other hand, God has the power to heal physical sickness as He was able to do with the deceased Lazarus.

3. **God Possesses the Power to Call**: Because God possesses the power to call, He called us out of sin, as He did Abraham (Gen.12). He called us into service, as He did Gideon. And, God can call us into sacrifice, as He did Stephen.

God has undiminished power!

A Decision That Delivers

Ultimately we must live with the consequences of our decisions. Decisions made solely on pleasure will lead to greater pain. Decisions made strictly on our happiness will lead to greater hurts. Decisions made on just reaping a financial profit will lead to spiritual and emotional bankruptcy. Only decisions made on God's purposes will lead to peace, promotion, and spiritual prosperity. **The greatest decision we can make is the decision to allow Jesus Christ to rule in our lives**. This decision will bring about a two-fold initiative. Furthermore, this decision will give us eternal life immediately (John 3:16) and it will eventually give us the enriched life (John 10:10).

Making Jesus Lord is an act of our will, a surrendering of our lives and a realization that we can do nothing without Him. This matter of Lordship has slipped out of the theology of the church. Yet, there is a strategic difference between the eternal and the enriched. The eternal life deals with light. The enriched life deals with liberty. The eternal life deals with place; the enriched life deals with power. The eternal life deals with standing; the enriched life deals with sitting. The eternal life deals with positional righteousness; the enriched life deals with practical rest. There are four reasons why Jesus has the right to rule in our lives.

1. **We are enriched by His Prophetic Person**. In Revelation 1:8 Jesus proclaims, "I am Alpha and Omega." Jesus is sovereign and supreme. He rules history. He predates time. He predetermines time and circumstances. He predestinates location. Jesus knows everything about our history, hurts, where we came from, everything we have been exposed to, every decision and failure. Jesus is Omnipresent (He is everywhere with His Allness), Omniscient (He knows everything from beginning to end), and Omnipotent (He is all-powerful: everything needs Jesus but Jesus needs nothing). We ought to let Him rule because we are enriched by His Person.

2. **We are enriched by His Preeminence**. Jesus rules the heavens and the universe. The purpose of God is a kingdom on earth that gives light and salt which will defeat the enemy. John says, in verse 12, that he sees the glorified Christ amongst the seven golden candlesticks (which represent the churches). As Jesus walks through the seven churches He holds the pastors

(the seven stars) in His hands. John's response was to "fall as dead at His feet" (v. 17). John falls because Jesus is preeminent. Yet, learning to put Him before everything is a process. He must come before our children, our hobbies, our recreation, our money, etc. Though it is hard to make Him first in everything, Jesus has the right to rule because He is preeminent.

3. **We are enriched by His Power**. Jesus rules Hell and the hopes of men. In Revelation 1:18 Jesus claims to have the "keys of Hell and the grave." Jesus has the right to choose who lives, who dies and when. Therefore, He has the right to rule over our lives.

4. **We are enriched by His Presence.** Jesus rules hearts. In John 21 we learn that Jesus helps us to find what we are really looking for. The apostles were fishing all night but caught nothing. Without Jesus we catch nothing. He has a right to rule in our lives because, once we buy into Jesus, we will find what we need. When Jesus confronted Peter He dealt with Peter's sense of failure, but He gives Peter focus: "feed my sheep."

When Jesus rules our hearts, there is a sense of His presence with confidence; we are courageous with a sense of calmness. When I have faith, I forsake all and trust Him. Forsaking my own ways, I trust Him; forsaking my history, I trust Him; forsaking my own rationale, I trust Him; forsaking this world, I trust Him. Jesus says, "If any man will come after Me, let him pick up his cross and deny himself and follow Me." **Jesus has the right to rule! Let Jesus rule!**

From Death to Dominion

The city of Jerusalem was under a tremendous hush as people cried out for Jesus of Nazareth to be crucified. They hung Him high as the good, the bad, and the ugly witnessed His crucifixion and death. As a result of His death, the disciples were dismantled, their joy was jolted, and the Prince of Peace was punished for proclaiming that He was the Son of God.

Jesus hung on the cross and gave up the Ghost. He died until the sun stopped shining and until a Roman Centurion was persuaded and said, *"Surely this was the Son of God."* The three days Jesus spent in the grave are crucial. The Passover Lamb, which had been transferred from judgment hall to judgment hall, had shed His blood. **Without the shedding of blood, there is no remission of sin.** Jesus accomplished 3 acts through His Passion.

1. **He Died.** The Gospel of Jesus Christ states that Jesus became our substitution. He died in our place. Colossians expresses the deity of Jesus Christ. He is God in the flesh. He created all things. He is the representative of the Godhead. He is the Alpha and Omega, Judge and Jury. He is a friend who comforts. As He preached on the cross, Jesus had seven last words. The sixth word was, "It is finished", which is the awesome plan of redemption. The demons did not want Jesus to die to redeem man. If Jesus had not gone to the cross, we would all be in hell. He disarmed spoiled principalities and powers. He ruined hell. He fulfilled Genesis 3:15. He crushed Satan's head. He declared He was God with power.

2. **He was Buried.** He Pre-empted and stripped the demons of their power. He ruined hell and rescued the hindered. He openly embarrassed Satan. More preachers need to tell the truth about what Jesus did for us. Forget prosperity, large congregations, speaking in other languages, and bringing attention to our names. Instead, we need to know about who Jesus is. We are sinners saved by grace, with a love we don't deserve, and a faith that is not our own, It is the gift of God, lest any man should boast.

3. **He Rose.** If Christ is not raised then we are most miserable. We are hell bound. We are without hope. *He got up with all power in His hands.* He Renewed the Broken Hearted. He met them on the mountain in Galilee with over five hundred people, He gave the great commission and announced that all power was in His hands. We no longer need a sacrifice. All we need to do is call

on the Name of Jesus and heaven opens up. God will hear our prayer and demons will tremble. "At the Name of Jesus, every knee shall bow and every tongue shall confess that Jesus is Lord to the Glory of God." He is not Mary's little baby. He is God Almighty. Just call on Jesus! There is power in His hand, power to live right, and power to talk right. As Philippians 3:10 says, "that I may know Him, and the power of His resurrection."

There is power in the Name of Jesus. *He has Power to save you, sanctify you and satisfy you.* He is the Beginning and the End, the Bright and Morning Star; He is our Savior. They put Him on the cross, but early on Sunday morning, He got up with All Power in His hands.

The Lord Is There

God's Glory is without a doubt, the greatest evidence of His deity. His Glory is His promotional device for His Presence. Without His Presence, there is no Glory. Without His Glory, there is no Presence. In His Glory are light, liberation, power, and peace. Since God's Glory is evidenced by a Presence, that Presence changes places throughout scripture. Ezekiel tells us where God's Presence resides. As we look at darkness, we see God's dominion. Ezekiel will tour with an angel who will show him prophetically, a vision; the Millennial Temple, which will take place on earth when Jesus Christ the Messiah returns. What we must learn from this chapter is that whenever there is a groan by God's people, God's Presence will bring Glory.

1. **The Glory of His Protection** (Exodus 40). The tabernacle of Moses, which was called, "The tent of meeting", was a temporary dwelling place for God. This tent was meaningful because it was there that the people worshipped God. There was movement when the Spirit of God was a cloud by day and a pillar fire by night; when the cloud moved they were to pack up the tent and move on. The Spirit of God in the gloom of persecution became their protection.

2. **The Glory of His Provision** (1 Kings 8:10-12). Solomon built a temple where the Shekinah Glory of God resided; it was for Israel's worship. God gave them provision concerning their poverty.

3. **The Glory of His Pardon** (Ezra 6). God reinstated the building of the temple. God placed it on the heart of an unsaved Gentile King to restore the house after the captivity. They restored the worship, but not the theocracy.

4. **The Glory of His Person** (St. John 2:19). Jesus is God's Glory. His person came to reverse the perversion of mankind. Jesus was born just in time because man was hell bound. Jesus came to save a dark and dying world.

5. **The Glory of His Program** (Ephesians 2:21). This is the entire church building. 1 Corinthians 3:16-17 tells us, the local church, that Jesus Christ dwells in us. He gives us the desire to live right. No weapon that is formed against you shall prosper. When the enemy comes in like a flood, the spirit of the Lord will

raise up a standard against him. You cannot take the temple of God (your body), and continue to fill it with carnality. The Spirit gives us the desire to want to do right. We are not perfect, but the Spirit does guide us to all truth.

6. **The Glory of God's Power** (Revelation 11). From the rapture to Armageddon, we hear the groan of the people and the glory of God's power. God used two witnesses to prove that He is still in control.

7. **The Glory of His Presence** (Ezekiel 40). Jesus is coming back to set up His earthly Kingdom where He will defeat the 666 (anti-Christ), and bind Satan for a thousand years. He will set up a Millennial Kingdom and rule with a rod of iron. He is King of kings and Lord of lords. If we are not saved, we will go to hell. Through Him, we have our life. He brings comfort and strength. When we feel like giving up, He shows up.

Creation groans and God brings His Glory, but as the saints groan; God brings deliverance. The Spirit groans when we utter and cannot pray. He understands the uttering we cannot understand. When He shows up, His presence will become our strength. When we cry, He sends peace, and power. *Thank God for the Glory that is in Jesus Christ!*

KNOWING HIM

That I may know Him, and the power of His resurrection, and the fellowship of His sufferings, being made conformable unto His death.

Philippians 3:10

Ingredients for Intimacy

Intimacy is a costly commodity which demands total sacrifice and total surrender of one's self and will. Intimacy is much more than physical closeness. A psychological oneness takes time. *You do not fall into love; you learn how to love.* Anything in the Bible with the word "fall" in it is bad. Whether you fall back or fall forward, it is bad.

Intimacy is a deep knowledge of another person. It is running the risk of being fully known by that other person. The reason some of us cannot become intimate is that we are wearing too many masks. Intimacy is where nothing is hidden and everything is exposed. Intimacy is to prioritize another before oneself. Intimacy includes serving, sacrificial loving and surrendering for the good of the relationship. When we look at the true meaning of intimacy, we do not measure up to it. We confuse physical closeness with spiritual closeness. *Physical closeness is enclosure. Intimacy is disclosure.* It is also the ability to know, nurture deeply, and run the risk of being known; taking off all of our masks and things that pump us up, for the good of the relationship. Intimacy with Jesus is a nurturing walk. Nothing can directly affect us when Jesus is in His proper place in our lives. He blocks harmful situations from us when we learn to trust, transfer, and have tranquility in who He is. In Phil: 3 the Apostle Paul is emphasizing the importance of having a spiritual mind:

1. **The Purpose** (V.3). We are set apart. We worship God in Spirit and we learn to rejoice in Jesus, having no confidence in our selves. In order to know God, we must know that God has incommunicable and communicable attributes.

2. **The Product** (V.15). Become fully mature in Christ. Things that used to hurt no longer have an affect on you. God wants His person to out-shine the problem. God has chosen to reveal Himself in Jesus, so that we may know Him on an intimate basis. The intimacy of God will perfect your peace. The closer we get to Jesus, the less things bother us.

3. **The Proposal** (vv.4-11). We must evaluate our gains and loses. Thus, we can abandon our plan, get close to Jesus, let Him run our life and learn to trust Him.

4. **The Perspective** (vv.12-13). Look at the past in the way God sees it. It was Grace and Mercy that brought us out. We need to change

our mind and our way of thinking, putting away our past method of reasoning.

5. **The Praise** (V.14). Paul exhorts us to "Press toward the mark, for the prize, of the high calling in Jesus Christ."

When we begin to get close to Jesus, He will start to affect our mind, money, and energy. Demons will start to back off, wayward children will come back, marriages will be made well, and you will sleep at night. This is asking Jesus to be Lord, deliverer, leader, and our power. "That I may know Him and the power of His resurrection."

Convinced: The Mysterious Garment

As Jesus died and was buried in a tomb, different accounts of His resurrection were rendered by various writers. Matthew reports a great earthquake when the angel of the Lord rolled back the stone. Mark says that when the women approached, they saw a young man sitting on the right side, clothed in a long white garment. Luke reports two men in shining garments, asking a question, *"Why seek ye the living among the dead?"* John is the only one who mentions grave clothes and two angels sitting; one at the

head and the other at the feet. When the woman started weeping, Mary, one of the women who came to the tomb, turned and saw Jesus standing, and "knew Him not". There are no contradictions; rather, **God knows what episode is needed in our lives in order to convince us of who He is**.

Therefore, each book of the Gospel is written from a different point of view.

Matthew included an earthquake, *Mark* included an angel, *Luke* included two angels in shining garments, *John and Peter* saw two angels and a change of mysterious clothing.

John and Peter needed more proof because John was going to point to Jesus as God, and Peter was the main pillar of the church. Let's examine the evidence: They saw that the clothes lay in place and the head napkin was not lying with the linen clothes, but wrapped together in a place by itself. In those days, the body of the dead was wrapped like a mummy.

Jesus had gone to Sheol, led out the captives, snatched the keys from Satan, closed up the paradise side of Hell, and waited around for 72 hours. Jesus did this in an inkling of a second, oozed through the clothes, sent for angels, walked the streets of Jerusalem, and then summoned a woman to find Him.

God has always convinced different people in different ways. He convinced Moses with a burning bush. He convinced Daniel with a passive Lion. He convinced David with a slingshot. He convinced Mary and Martha with a fake funeral. He convinced Paul along the Damascus road - but **are you convinced**?

God's Delays Are Not Dismissals

 Our evaluation of God is foolishness because God is infinite and we are finite. His ways are not our ways and His thoughts are not our thoughts. In fact, *we cannot interpret His purposes because we do not have the power of comprehension to define and understand the workings of God.* In Romans 8, The Apostle Paul has been arguing for the believer's security. God has a plan and a purpose, and nothing will interfere, stop, or pause the purposes of God. In Romans chapter 9, Paul wants us to see that God's delays are never dismissals. God always comes back to deal with us. He never leaves us nor forsakes us.

1. **God's Character is His Faithfulness** (vv.1-13).The blinding and rejection of Israel caused us (the Gentiles), to get saved. We have the privilege of His Son-ship (adoption), His presence, His promises, and the law. When we are in sin and out of fellowship with God, He still has something to say. His foreknowledge has allowed this as a part of His plan. Our destiny cannot be altered. There may be some delay, but He will work even through our sin. Satan will not bother the unsaved because he already has them. If you are going to be glorified with Christ, you must suffer with Him (1st Peter 2). We did not choose Jesus, He chose us. In fact, some of us are worse than the unsaved.

2. **God's Choosing is His Righteousness** (vv.14-18). God does what He wants to do. No one has the right to question His decisions. His decisions are righteous. God draws people through the perfections of Christ and through Hell fire. In spite of all that we have done, God still loves us.

3. **God's Control is His Justice** (vv.19-29). Why does God find fault with man? This is the condition of the clay; we are the clay, and Jesus is the Potter. We are in the Potter's hand. Although we have intellect and a will, who can resist God when He lifts us up? When we are in God's hand we do not choose our own gifts, ministry, direction, or our burdens. In the Potter's hand, He does whatever He wants to do for His own Glory. We have no power over ourselves. Jesus has all the power. He has jurisdiction over every thing in our lives. He makes decisions as to how long our trials will last, how long our suffering will last, the pace of our growth, and the process of our sanctification. God is in control. When we learn that Jesus is in control, we will have joy no matter what Satan sends in our lives. God determines who will be elected. We cannot resist when we are elected. God determines whether man will be a Moses or a Pharaoh. Man cannot choose his birth, race, or ethnicity. God does what He wants to do. He is sovereign.

4. **God's Compassion is His Grace** (vv.30-33). Whatever delays God has placed in our life, it is not the final decision. God may choose to do other things while we are waiting on Him. God may not come when we want Him, but He is always on time. Jesus is able to stop and help someone else before He gets to us. We cannot ever doubt that He is coming back to help us. Whatever we have prayed for, we must believe that we have already received it. God has not forgotten us. *God's delays are not always dismissals, but sometimes God's delays are our deliverances.* "They that wait upon the Lord shall renew their strength." Our delays may be to increase our faith, to help us to depend on Jesus, and to mature us to grow in Him. To God be the Glory. The Lord is faithful!

Lessons Learned by Listening to God

In Christendom, there is a rule for the righteous, a lesson for learning, a help to the hurting, and an answer for the afflicted. Only those who are able to listen to God are liberated from the entanglements of Satan. The Bible has many illustrations of people who moved ahead of God; who used Him for conveniences only and abandoned Him later. People seeking freedom without faith, riches without righteousness, pleasures without principles, and triumphs without truth, will be subjected to repeating the same mistakes. If you move without the Master, you have already been defeated. We must not proceed without prayer and not commit without God's counsel. Satan will come to you as a roaring lion, and as a serpent, subtly, to disrupt you.

In the context of Joshua chapter 9, Joshua has seen the promotion and the preemption of God. After all Joshua went through, he should have immediately recognized something that was not of God. Jericho represents the flesh, Aí represents the world system. The Gibeonites represent the devil. We will see three things Satan provides for us when we don't listen to God.

1. **False Covering** (vv.1-6). Satan has a lying motive and mechanism. His plan is to get close to you to deceive you. There are people in the church who come regularly, but are not of the church. They have a false covering. Satan has many disguises and he wants to catch us off-guard. He lied to Eve, but he deceived Adam. He wants to get our sights off of God. The people wanted Joshua to make a decision without praying and without God's direction. If you continue in the ways of the world, you will get into something and you will not be able to get out.

2. **Fictitious Communication** (vv.7-11). Israel's communication became fabricated because their covering was false. Learn to hear not only what people say, but what they do not say. The Gibeonites tried to make a false agreement with Joshua. They lied about their country, commodity, clothing, consecration, and their comradeship. Joshua was trying to be merciful to these people, but they were lying to him.

3. **Failing Covenant** (V.12). Every time we move without God we will fail. The Israelites started murmuring amongst themselves. The move separated the Nation of Israel. Movement was made without the Master. Confusion will come the moment we enter into a covenant with Satan. We cannot eat the delicacies of the

world and expect no consequences to come back to us. We serve a Holy God who will convict and convert us. We cannot be in the world and of the world. We cannot loose our eternal life, but our liberty will leave when we let Satan plant his seed.

We cannot let Satan deceive us. The purpose of God's discipline is to cause us not to go back to where we came from. When you wait on God, wisdom will come and bring us to the point of His mercy. His mercy is new every morning. In spite of us, God has been good. The goodness of God leads us to repentance. Mercy saved us and put us on the straight path. Don't move without God.

Mandatory Mail

Basic training is difficult for soldiers because they are being prepared for possible warfare. Mail-call is pleasurable because the soldier receives mail from home. Oftentime, the mail has two major components, intimacy and instruction. John, in approximately 90-95 AD, writes the letter of I John to the churches. It is an intimate letter because it is from a pastoral perspective, but it is also a polemic (passionate arguement), because John is on the defense. John wants to get back to the basics of basic training. John wants to authenticate and substantiate what it really means to be saved. He also wants us to walk in truth and not follow a lie. Thus, in the letter called 1 John, John deals with fellowship.

1. **The Person of the Fellowship**. John answers the question, how do I know I am in fellowship with God? John immediately begins to attack a doctrinal error (Gnosticism), that has slipped into the church. This error denied both the deity and humanity of Jesus. John produced two tests to authenticate our salvation and our walking in truth. These tests concern doctrine. The first test deals with a Biblical view of Jesus. The second test deals with the doctrine of sin. If we pass these two tests, we may be assured of our salvation and that we are walking in truth. *Test #1* deals with the Biblical view of Jesus. It is about the incarnation. In the first three verses of I John chapter 1, John speaks about what he and others had heard, seen, and handled with their hands. Since the Gnostics believed Jesus was a spirit, John's attack deals with proving Jesus' humanity. Jesus had to be a man because we cannot see or feel a spirit.

Jesus came out of eternality into time. Jesus added humanity without diminishing His divinity. He is one hundred percent man and one hundred percent God, the hypostatic union. Incarnation brought on imputation. Imputation is the belief that our righteousness is imputed from Jesus. None of us are righteous. When Jesus died on the cross, He imputed His righteousness to our account. Now God does not see us, He sees Jesus. We have eternal life because of that fact. The person of this fellowship is Christ, who is fully man and fully God. If we believe this; we have passed the first test.

2. **The Peace of our Fellowship**. We have intimacy with Jesus. Intimacy means that we are abiding in the vine and walking with Him. My will is His will; my wisdom is His wisdom; my work is His work. The more we walk with Jesus, the more our joy becomes full. Jesus brings deliverance, which brings peace in our fellowship.

3. **The Prerequisite for Fellowship**. *Test #2* has to do with our view of sin. When we have a claim that compromises the Word, it is a lie. I John 1:5 tells us "God is light, and in Him is no darkness at all. If we say that we have fellowship with Him, and walk in darkness, we lie, and do not know the truth (V.6). But if we walk in the light, as He is in the light, we have fellowship one with another, and the blood of Jesus Christ, His Son cleanseth us from all sin. (V.7). If we say that we have no sin, we deceive ourselves, and the truth is not in us" (V.8).

We fail the second test if we claim to have no sin because that compromises the Word. According to the Word of God, If we claim to have no sin we are lying. However, when we say the same thing God says about our sin, we have forgiveness. John writes so that we will not sin, but if we sin, we have a lawyer (2:1), who is Jesus. When we confess our sins, Jesus turns to the Father and shows His nail-prints. God the Father forgives our sin because Jesus paid the price for the penalty of our sins.

Did you pass these tests? If you passed them both, you are saved and walking in truth.

Trusting God in Trying Times

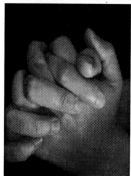

Joshua, the son of Nun, was a slave in Egypt, a servant who knew how to serve God (I Chronicles 7:27), a soldier that slew the Amalekites (Exodus 1:7), a faithful spy, and a man that had a resume' of righteousness. Our greatest fulfillment in life should be when we are in the place of God. If we are not in the right place, we will not receive the promises of God. The land of Canaan is a picture of inheritance. In order to get to our inheritance we must face battles before the blessings.

God prepared us years ago for what He wants us to do right now. Jeremiah tells us that He called him, sanctified him, and ordained him as a prophet. Likewise, everything in our life is apart of God's will to bring us to where He wants us. God has even allowed our mistakes. He is too wise to make a mistake in our lives. In the context of Joshua, we will examine his commission.

1. **A New Directive** - (God's Perspective). You cannot lead until you learn to listen to God (Psalm 32:8). Do not try to go into a plan without prayer. God has a purpose and He wants His people to participate in it. The church is not a place for fraternities and sororities. The purpose of the church is to exalt Jesus Christ. God chose Joshua after Moses died and God gave him a new plan. God's plan has been set for our inheritance. We had nothing to do with it.

2. **A New Direction** - (God's Provision). God told Joshua to be strong. In the Old Testament, prosperity was associated with being in the place of God. God will bless us as we get into the place, purpose, power, and peace of God.

3. **A New Deployment** - (God's Protection, Purpose, and Promises.) You are in His purposes. Success with God comes through keeping His Word. God has blessed many of us, and as we help with the ministry of the church, God will continue to help us and our families. However, many of us are not involved in the purpose of God's plan.

4. **A New Deliverance** - (God's Presence: Peace, Power, and Provision). If God is with us, He is more than the whole world against us. Joshua heard from God (V.10) and obeyed. When we are in God's plan, we will be blessed. He will provide battles just to keep us humble. Going across our "Jordan" means to make up in our mind to be in the will of God, crucify our flesh, and move into the Spirit. There is no victory until we make this decision within our minds. We will be blessed when we walk in the light and live a life of obedience. His priority is our inheritance, which is His promise.

Are you in the position to receive His promises? We must be in the right place to be blessed. We must be willing to do God's will in order to experience God's wealth; Investing in His vision. He wants His people promoted when they demonstrate obedience to His Word.

Husbands, you must love your wives as Christ loved the Church. Wives, you must be respectful to your husbands. Children, you must obey your parents. Tithe and stop tipping God. Be obedient to the Word of God. He will do far, exceedingly, and abundantly above all that you can ask or think!

All scripture is given by inspiration of
God, and is profitable for doctrine,
for reproof, for correction,
for instruction in righteousness.
2 Timothy 3:16

Doom of the Wrong

The requisites for responding to God's requirements for building His Church are steep. The individual must be completely sold out for the Kingdom, and not concerned with the pay or benefits. He must be willing to stand in the face of opposition. It is with this understanding that Paul writes his letter of encouragement to Timothy, his son in the faith, who was timid and afraid.

The theme of I Timothy is Church order. It deals with the protocol and the practices in the Church. Paul confronts the issues of false teachers, public worship, qualifications of leaders and then gives Timothy personal instruction. Paul outlines care for the widows and provides instruction to slaves. Chapter one begins with an exhortation for sound doctrine. It addresses the legislation, the lie, and the law.

1. **The Legislation**: Paul opens this letter establishing his God-given authority. He was appointed by commandment of God (I Tim 1:1). After establishing his authority, Paul shares the legislation: teach sound doctrine! The Church was being bombarded with unbiblical doctrines that attacked the deity of Jesus Christ and His incarnation. Paul charged and cautioned Timothy to adhere to sound doctrine. *Understanding the importance of sound doctrine is critical to our effectiveness as believers, as we will ultimately live out what we believe.* Sound doctrine is rooted in God, as He is the source of all righteousness, through His Word, He reveals that our redemption is solely in Him. Because of man's total depravity, reconciliation to God the Father comes from the finished work of Jesus Christ alone. Once redemption and reconciliation occur, reformation follows. Reformation of man comes through the power of the Holy Spirit working in our lives. He is the only one who can change us, and He will do what is necessary to conform us into the image of Christ.

    Paul's charge for Timothy was to steadfastly, rightly divide the Word of truth. He was charged to interpret the Holy Spirit's leading through the Word of God. The Holy Spirit never leads us contrary to the Word of God. God speaks through His Word. "God who at sundry times and in divers manners spake in times past by the prophets, Hath in these last days spoken unto us by His Son" (Heb 1:1).

23

2. **The Lie**: Paul cautions Timothy not to get caught up in the lie. We need to take heed to sound doctrine and not get caught up in fables, superstitions, foolish talking, or anything that is outside the realm of faith. We cannot base our beliefs upon our experiences, or the experiences of others. Anything that is not inside the realm of faith detracts from the exaltation of Jesus Christ and is a lie. Jesus is truth.

3. **The Law**: Finally, Paul deals with the law. There are those who desire to teach the law, but they don't understand what they say. The law is good if a man uses it lawfully. Laws are not for the righteous; they exist to keep unrighteous men in order. We must ignore the lie and understand the purpose of the laws. We must base our life on the truth of the Word of God, which is rooted in Jesus Christ. He is our Redeemer, Reconciler, and Reformer.

Examination to Exoneration

Autopsies are requested by the medical examiner's office when the death of an individual is in question. This examination is a procedure where trained doctors open the body of the deceased to determine the cause of death. In a similar sense, Dr. Jesus Christ examines the Church as He stands in the midst of the candlesticks. He examines the function, the failures, the faithfulness, and the fruit of each Church.

The seven churches of Revelation 2 and 3 are representative of all churches. They also represent church ages. And, they represent the individual, for He says, He who has an ear, let him hear. John has a format for each church. It includes four critical elements: Jesus' commendation, condemnation, counsel, and caution.

1. **Ephesus** (representing the Apostolic Age from AD 60 to100). Jesus (the One who holds the seven stars in His right hand and walks in the midst of the seven golden candlesticks), gives a commendation (Rev. 2:2-3). He knows that they are a serving, sacrificial, steadfast, and suffering church. Nevertheless, they had left their first love (the condemnation). In other words, their labor could not replace their love. Jesus counsels them to remember (get back to the first time they had met Him) and repent (return to the place where they ought to be). Finally, He cautions them. He says that the one who overcomes (the truly saved), will eat of the tree of life.

2. **Smyrna** (representing the period of persecution from AD 100 to 300). Jesus identifies Himself as the First and the Last, which was dead and is now alive. Jesus knows that they have been under persecution and He commends them for refusing to compromise what they believe. He counsels and cautions them that for a short time, some will be put into prison, but Jesus will give them the victor's crown.

3. **Pergamos** (representing the period of church-wide imperial favor from AD 315 to 500). Jesus identifies Himself as the One who has the sharp two-edged sword (Rev. 2:12). Jesus commends them because they were diligent. Yet, they compromised with the devil (condemnation). He counsels them to repent. He cautions them that, if they hear what the Spirit says to them, He will give them a white stone (representing freedom from judgment), and a new name.

25

4. **Thyatira** (represented by a church/state religion from AD 500 to 1500). Jesus identifies Himself as the One who judges (He has eyes like a flame of fire). He commends them for their deeds, love, faith, service, and perseverance. Yet, He condemns them for allowing false religions to come into the church. He counsels them that sickness is on the way because they are persisting in their sin. Jesus counsels and cautions those who have not been overcome to hold fast until He comes.

5. **Sardis** (represented by the period of the Reformation). Jesus is identified as having the seven Spirits of God and the seven stars. Jesus commends only a few for not soiling their garments, and walking with Him. He then condemns most of the church for not doing His will. To the ones who overcome, He counsels and cautions that they will be clothed in white garments. He will not erase their names from the book of life, and He will confess their names before His Father.

6. **Philadelphia** (the true church). Jesus identifies Himself as the One who is holy and true. There is no condemnation for this church, only a commendation. They have kept His Word, and have not denied His Name (Rev. 3:8). Jesus knows that Satan has plans to come after them, but He tells them not to worry because He is going to rearrange Satan's plans. Finally, He counsels them to hold fast because He is coming quickly.

7. **Laodicea** (the church of today). This church receives no commendation but a condemnation. He knows their deeds, they are neither cold nor hot. Jesus does not want us lukewarm (half worldly and half in Christ). Jesus is speaking to the church when He cautions them saying, "Behold, I stand at the door (of our hearts) and I am knocking; if any man hear my voice let him open the door and I will come into him and sup with him, and he with Me." Jesus is not really in their hearts, for they are a pretentious church.

Under examination we find that we were doomed; we were dead; we were hell bound, but God, who is rich in mercy, gave us His grace. God's grace brought us exoneration. The grace of God ought to make us live pure, live a life pleasing to the Lord, and it ought to open up the door to what joy is. We can't have joy, shout, or live lives that are pure and pleasing until we understand grace. It is not until we know that God has been good that we can have joy.

God's Method of Operation

As we became saved, we passed through a succession of divine operations. These are designed by God to deliver us from our Adamic nature, which we inherited simply because we are part of the human race. Our nature encompasses all of the experiences and mind-sets we have been exposed to since birth. God uses a system of death and resurrection to give the born-again believer power over sin.

God's system of death renders our Adamic nature powerless, as we grow in the Word, and yield to God. God's system of resurrection gives us a new Godly capacity to live out a righteous life before God. When we as Believers are born-again, we actually die. The word "death," simply means <u>separation</u>. Physical death is separation from the body while spiritual death is separation from God. When we accept <u>Jesus Christ</u> as our personal Savior, we become dead to the demands of our old natures.

The apostle Paul, in Galatians 2, tells us of the argument which the Galatian cities used in order to try to overthrow his doctrine, and the argument which he used to overthrow their doctrine. The cities' argument against Paul is that justification by Faith in Christ only, apart from the word of the law, is a highly dangerous doctrine. It totally weakens a man's sense of moral responsibility. By saying a man can be accepted through trusting in Christ without any necessity to do good works, Paul is encouraging men to break the law, which leads to sin. Paul's entire argument, however, is that once a person is united with God, he/she is never the same person again. Instead, they are changed – radically changed.

Paul describes this change by using the term "death" and "life". Twice in V.19- 20, he speaks of dying and being raised to life again. Both take place through union with Christ. Once we are united with <u>Jesus Christ</u>, we can never really go back. He gives us new desires for holiness, for God, and for Heaven. It is not that we cannot sin again, we can, however, we do not want to. It is in V.20 that Paul deals with this process of death and resurrection; each step specifies a different doctrinal process that we pass through.

There are four processes:
1) **Condemnation and Death:**
   I am crucified with Christ (Rom. 6:1-6, I Cor. 12:13).
2) **Justification:**
   Nevertheless, I live (Rom. 3:24).

3) **Imputation**:
   Not I, but Christ that liveth in me (Rom. 5).
4) **Sanctification:**
   I live by the faith of the Son of God (Gal. 2:20).

We are dead *TO* sin, but not dead *FROM* sin.

When God saves us, all He asks is that we have faith. John says that we overcome by faith – the work is <u>finished</u>. All we need is faith - "Faith cometh by hearing the Word of God." As we stay in the Word, our faith is increased, our minds are renewed, our attitudes are cleansed, we desire to walk in the light, and we become full of joy.

God is operating on us! <u>First</u>, He gave us a heart transplant that changed our emotions and radically altered our wills. <u>Second</u>, He performed brain surgery on us through His Word. He is renewing our minds. We think differently because we have a *single* mind to live for Christ. We have a *submissive* mind, "Let this mind be in you which was also in <u>Christ Jesus</u>." We have a *spiritual* mind because we are forgetting those things which are behind. We have a *secure* mind, doing everything by prayer and supplication, letting all requests be made known unto the Lord. "I can do all things through Christ who strengthens me." <u>Third</u>, He has also completed a foot operation. We walk differently; we walk in the light. <u>Fourth</u>, He gave us oral surgerys; We talk differently.

The Lord Jesus Christ is operating daily. We can feel His anesthesia of love. We can feel His dose of conviction and we can feel His comfort of recovery. Every time He operates, we are a little closer to being like Jesus. "I am crucified with Christ, nevertheless I live. Not I, but Christ who lives within me" (Gal. 2:20).

Habakkuk

The Power of Praising God in Poverty

One of the awesome feats of a Believer is when maturity in Christ has promoted us to see the Lord. People normally are only able to praise God when they can see and experience His blessings. However, for every mountain there is a valley; for every elevation there is a corresponding declension. Many times we are only able to thank God and rejoice over what is *prospering* in our lives. Please don't misunderstand me, we ought to exalt our Lord for all of His benefits, the food on our tables, the clothes on our backs, the roof over our heads, but there are times when God solicits our praise solely based on who He is.

Habakkuk may have witnessed the decline and fall of the Assyrian empire and the rise of the Babylonian Kingdom near the end of the seventh century B.C. The book of Habakkuk takes the form of a dialogue between God and the prophet. Habakkuk observes that the leaders in Judah are oppressing the poor so he raises the question, "why does God allow these wicked people to prosper"? Then God assures him that the Chaldaeans will come to punish Judah. Habakkuk becomes more concerned. How can justice prevail when the wicked Chaldaeans, who are actually worse than the wicked Jews, are allowed by God to bring judgment upon God's chosen people? God's reply is that the "just shall live by faith" in God and have the confidence that God is doing what is right. The book can be broken down by chapters. Chapters 1 and 2 discuss Habakkuk's doubts, while chapter 3 speaks about shouts of praise.

The soul of the prophet is Encouraged. (Habakkuk 3:2)
The eyes of the prophet are Enlightened . (3:3-16)
The heart of the prophet is Enriched. (3:18)
The feet of the prophet are Enabled. (3:19)

In V.17, the prophet is shown a picture. In the picture, *God allows pressures and pitfalls before He brings provisions.*

If It Doesn't Fit, You Must Get Rid of It

When we use a key to unlock a door, it has to fit exactly or it will not turn to disengage the lock. All of us have experienced having keys that look authentic but in actuality cannot open the door. In a similar sense, there are many beliefs and other faiths that appear authentic on the surface but, in reality, they cannot open the door of truth found in all 66 books of the Bible.

In the first five verses of Galatians 3, Paul argues from his personal experience. He experiences God, the Son, in V.1, who saves him. He experiences God the Holy Spirit in vv.2- 4 who will sanctify him, and he experiences God the Father in V.5, who sanctions the miracles and special blessings in his life.

Now Paul makes a transition and he is arguing from Old Testament scripture in vv.6-14. Since the Judaizers bragged about Abraham and the Law, Paul decides to argue from the Old Testament position of Abraham and the law to prove the point that salvation is by faith and not by works. He uses four dynamics to prove his point:

1. **The Pardon of God** (vv.6-7). Essentially, Paul demonstrates how God pardons sinners. In Genesis 15:6, Galatians 3:6, Romans 4:11 The Word *accounted* means *imputed*. Paul shows that when we get saved, God imputes our sins to another's account (Jesus Christ) and His Righteousness becomes ours. Paul reminded the Judaizers not to get caught up in their genealogy from Abraham because every man must come to salvation for himself, because God does not have grandchildren.

2. **The People that God will Save** (vv.8-9). The word *heathen* means *Gentiles*. God promised Abraham that in him all the nations would be blessed. God gave Abraham personal promises, national promises, political promises, unusual promises and spiritual promises. The greatest promise that emerged from Abraham's seed was Christ.

3. **The Process of Salvation is by Faith not the Law** (vv.10-12). Paul quotes Habakkuk 2:4, "The just shall live by faith." God's process has always been by faith never works. The law can never justify a sinner, neither can it give him righteousness. Nobody can live by the law because the law kills and brings guilt, however, we are freed by the operation of faith.

4. **The Person of Salvation is Christ** (vv.13-14). Christ redeemed us with His precious blood and set us free. The book of Deuteronomy says, "cursed is everyone who is hanged on a tree. Jesus set us free! He removes our curse and He saves us.

30

Is There Any Order in the House?

Universal order is one the strongest assertions of the existence of God. The heavens declare His glory. Creation screams out that there is a God somewhere. He keeps order in heaven and in hell. God hates disorder; It is a sign of chaos. Even the Godhead: God the Father, God the Son, and God the Holy Spirit, exist in a divine order. Concerning the creation, God the Father thought it, God the Son bought it and God the Holy Spirit sealed it. Everything associated with God is orderly.

During the first century there were three major problems concerning church order that Paul deals with in I Timothy 2.

1. **Prayer**. Paul opens with an exhortation to pray: "I exhort therefore, that first of all, supplications, prayers, intercessions, and giving of thanks be made for all men" (I Tim. 2:1). He is addressing the primacy of prayer in the local church. Contextually his exhortation is to men; however, every believer ought to have a consistent prayer life. He outlines four different types of prayers. *Supplications* are requests for a perceived need. *Prayers* address our worship and reverence for God. *Intercessions* are petitions on behalf of someone else. *Thanks* are expressions of gratitude.

   The particular things we should pray for are outlined in verse 2: "For kings and all those in authority." When we pray for those who are in authority, it is pleasing to God" (V.3). We have an obligation to pray for political leaders, pastors, bosses, and all those who are in a position of authority.

   As we make prayer a priority, and we pray for people, we must pray in the name of the right person. There is only one person who can speak on our behalf. "For there is one God, and one mediator between God and men, the man Jesus Christ" (V.5). He is the person who can speak on our behalf because He made the payment: "gave himself a ransom for all" (V.6). He purchased us out of the marketplace of sin. Paul includes his personal plea, stating that the only reason for which he exists is to preach the gospel of Christ.

   Prayer must be done in purity. Men who are holy should be lifting up their hands in confidence toward God without wrath or doubt (V.8). Sin must be identified and confessed in order to have an effective prayer life.

2. **The Persona of Women in Church**. Paul makes a transition from prayer to the persona of women in the local church. He deals with the submission of women within the local body. The requirements of dress for women are that they be clothed in modest and decent apparel. Women should be dressed in a manner that becomes godliness (V.9). Paul is specifying how a woman in the local church should look. If modesty in dress is not practiced, it can become a stumbling block to the men in church.The next issue he addresses concerning women is how she ought to learn. She ought to learn in a peaceable manner, not arguing or contending (V.11). Women ought to learn and lecture in a certain manner. "But I suffer not a woman to teach, nor to usurp authority over the man, but to be in silence" (V.12). Women can not allow the feminist movement to infiltrate and disrupt order in the local church.

3. **The Place of Women in Church**. Paul goes on to lay out the reason for the structure in the local church. "For Adam was first formed, then Eve" (V.13). Satan was able to deceive the woman (V.14). God's structure leads to His strategy. Women are not to lord over men in the Church; instead a woman's power lies in her effective management of the home. "Notwithstanding, she shall be saved in childbearing, if they continue in faith and charity and holiness with sobriety" (V.15) Women must not get caught up in fighting for women's rights, but instead, ensure that she is taking her rightful place.

Order in the local church requires the effective leading of holy men who will pray for those in authority, and women willing to submit to God's order.

Job

An <u>Avalanche</u> is a fall or slide of a large mass of snow, rock or other material down a mountainside. Step into the time tunnel with me, and let's travel together back to the land of Uz. This land, had a citizen, who had the respect of everyone. He was blameless, upright, God-fearing, and clean-living. His very name was a synonym for integrity and godliness. His name was Job, and he had 10 children, fields of livestock, an abundance of land, a household of servants and a substantial stock of cash.

Then without announcement, adversity thundered upon him, like an avalanche of giant, jagged rocks. He lost his children, livestock, land, servants, cash: and soon thereafter, Job lost his health. How could he ward off bitterness or impending thoughts of suicide? There are three possible answers.

1. **Job Claimed God's Loving Rights of Sovereignty** (Job 1:21). He sincerely believed God had a right to take away what He gave him (2:10). He looked up claiming His Lord's right to rule over his life.

2. **Job Looked to the Resurrection of the Redeemed**. "I know that my Redeemer lives and at the last day I shall see God." (Job. 19:25) Job looked ahead. Paul says in Romans 5, "Hope maketh not ashamed; because the Love of God is shed abroad in our hearts." He looked ahead for a change to come and He looked ahead for his redeemer to show up.

3. **Job Acknowledged his Lack of Knowledge** (Job 6:24). What a relief this brings! Job didn't feel obligated to explain the why's of the situation "Trust in the Lord with all thine heart, and lean not to thine own understanding" (Prov. 3:5). He looked within confessing his inability to put it all together, and resting his case with the righteous judge. Are we feeling the avalanche of falling rocks or maybe it has already fallen? We must pick up the pieces by faith.

Our lives must go through a series of tests and it is always our faith that enables us to finish the race (agony) that is set before us. "Looking unto Jesus, the Author and Finisher of our Faith." (Heb. 12:2).

Matthew 21:10

One of the greatest ploys ever to emerge in the film industry was that of concealing the identity of a character. For example, the idenities of the Lone Ranger, Zorro, Batman and Superman were often kept secret until the end of the story. Spiritually, as the Logos (Word of God), became flesh and tabernacled among us, many people only saw the human side of <u>Christ</u>. To them, Jesus' true idenity was hidden. Similarly, today many still only see Jesus as a man; however, He is the embodiment of the <u>God-Head</u>.

Jesus and His disciples approached Jerusalem, prior to His crucifixion, Jesus sent two of His disciples to find a donkey and a colt. This ride was the fulfillment of Old Testament prophecy of Zech. 9:9. *(Kings rode to war on horses; but they rode in peace on donkeys.)*

The Book of Matthew presents Jesus Christ as the Anointed Messiah, the King of Israel and the seed of David. In Matthew chapter 21, Jesus is making a last effort to present Himself to the nation of Israel, but instead they rejected Him. The Jews began to resent Him. They rejected at least six aspects of Jesus Christ; and for every outward rejection of Jesus, there was a corresponding inward deficiency: They rejected His prophecy because they were blind. They rejected His praise (vv.6-9) because they were baffled. They rejected His person (vv.10,11) because they were bitter. They rejected His purification (vv.12,13) because they were bad. They rejected His popularity (V.14) because they were boastful. They rejected His power (V.23) because they were in bondage.

They rejected Him because they did not <u>know</u> Him – blind, baffled, bitter, bad and boastful people are always in bondage. "Who is He, and what is He to you?" Colossians 1 reveals that He is the Image of the invisible God, the first born over all creation and that all things were created by Him and for Him.

There are seven testimonies given in God's Word: <u>The Seas of Galilee Testified</u>: He is a storm breaker. He holds the keys to the doctrine of aquatics as He walked on water. <u>The Five Loaves of Bread Testified</u>: He can reproduce food without producing a harvest. <u>The Grave-Yard Testified</u>: He can drive divine order in reverse, when He reversed death back to life. <u>Blindness Testified</u>: He can break through darkness by creating perfected light. <u>A Mountain Testified</u>: He can change Himself into a cosmic glow in a moment and return to a human without any after-effects. <u>A Tomb Testified</u>: He can leave His burial place without exerting any energy. <u>Hell Testified</u>: He can walk into

Sheol and by His mere presence crush Satanic powers. However, the greatest testimony is when we testify. We were sinking deep in sin, but He found me, He saved me, He lifted me, He sanctified me and He strengthened me.

Method of Confirmation

Whenever a manufacturer wants to test a product, he subjects that product to a series of tests. These tests are designed to verify the capability and durability of the product. However, if the product begins to experience problems, there is a manufacturer's manual designed to explain how the product is designed to work, and how the product is to be repaired.

Spiritually, God is the manufacturer of the entire universe, and He allows both His Church and His children to undergo a series of tests designed to bring them into maturity, direction, and devotion to Him. Whenever there is a defect, it is His will for us to return to His manual for instruction and direction.

1. **Paul's Confession to the Jews** (Galatians 2:1-2). Paul used God's Word to verify his work (V.2). That is why everything we do or plan to do must be in line with God's will. It is easy to make determinations based on our own understanding. The Israelites based their determinations on the bad report given by the 10 spies (Numbers 13). Paul was always led by the Spirit to the scriptures.

2. **Paul's Claim to the Jews** (Galatians 2:3-5; Acts 15:6-21). Jews had a hard time with the religious barriers, walls, or partitions being broken down. They could not believe that in <u>Christ</u>, there are no racial, social or religious differences. James concluded, in his book, that false brethren were causing the divisions.

   Satan has people in place, people who externally appear on-board, but Satan can, at any time, control their rationale, thinking and emotions. These people, who are not internally yielded to the Holy Spirit, do not even know or understand how they are being used. They operate through the flesh and rely on their rationale. Consequently, their thinking is not based on scripture.

3. **Paul's Confirmation to the Jews** (II Timothy 2:6-10). The Judaizer had hoped to get the leaders of the Jerusalem church to disagree with Paul. Paul made it clear that he was not impressed or moved by one's "person" or "position". He respected them, but was willing to fight for the authority of God's Word. Through the Word of God, Paul confirmed His work, His will, and His way. Look at the results: the right hand of fellowship was extended

to him (which was a sign of agreement and trust that God had endorsed their decision), and support was rendered. In other words, God endowed peace.

Whenever we are faced with uncertainty or if we are struggling with issues, we must make a decision to go back to God's manufacturer's manual. Remember, Jesus said, "If you abide in my word, you are my disciples and you shall know the truth, and the truth shall make you free." Free from deception, bondage, feelings, rationale, self and Satan.

The Power of God's Timing

The preparation and passion of the Passover week was a pivotal point in the life and ministry of Jesus Christ. The Triumphal Entry was a timed event. It was another proof that God has a perfect plan. He is sovereign, all wise, and exercising His power to plan. He has the answer before the question is posed.

Jesus is the Passover Lamb. He is the pure, undefiled Lamb without blemish. He timed Himself so that He would be in Jerusalem four days ahead of time. Chapter 12 of St. John opens with Jesus having dinner with Lazarus, whom He had raised from the dead. Mary anointed His feet with expensive ointment as an act of worship. This served as a memorial and preparation for His crucifixion. Jesus replied to Judas, who complained about the use of this expensive ointment: "Let her alone: against this day of my burying hath she kept this" (V.7).

The purpose for Christ's entry to Jerusalum, is revealed in verses 13-19. The same Jesus who had raised Lazarus from the dead, was now entering Jerusalem on an ass' colt. His timing of raising Lazarus and entering Jerusalem ensured that He would have witnesses. He invites the witnesses and then incites the leadership. They cried out, "Hosanna!" (which means save now). They wanted to be saved from Roman rule. His purpose was not to rule, but to die. He came as a lamb, not as a lion.

1. **The Plan**: Jesus had a following, which threatened the leadership and incited them to jealousy. As a result, they sought to kill him. Jesus invites them, knowing that they will reject him. "But Israel he saith, All day long I have stretched forth my hands unto a disobedient and gainsaying people" (Romans 10:21). The Jewish leaders cooperated with God's plan. It was His plan to die. "The hour is come, that the Son of Man should be glorified" (John 12:23).

2. **The Payment**: The payment was Jesus' life. He died that we could have life and life more abundantly. If we are willing to die to ourselves, fruit comes forth. "Except a corn of wheat fall into the ground and die, it abideth alone but if it dies, it bringeth forth much fruit" (John 12:24). He lays out incentives for the believer to be sold out for Him. If we are willing to give up our life, we gain life.

3. **The Pain**: The payment did not come without pain. Jesus cried, "Now is my soul troubled save me from this hour but for this

cause came I unto this hour" (John 12:27). Trouble in the life of the believer has a purpose. Jesus knew He would have to experience great pain; however, the purpose for which He came was greater than the pain. "Father glorify thy name" (John 12:28). "And I, if I be lifted up from the earth, will draw all men unto me" (John 12:32).

Jesus is the Passover Lamb. He fulfilled His purpose. He executed His plan. He made the payment and was willing to experience the pain so that the Father would be glorified, and man would be redeemed.

Speak When the Spirit Specifies

One of the evidences of God's presence, power, and peace, is God's order. God's presence brings comfort. God's power brings conquering compassion. God's peace brings divine control. Thus, in Paul's first letter to the Corinthians, he speaks of God as a God of order and not a God of confusion. Wherever there is confusion, God is not in the vicinity. This order is reflective and indicative of God working in and throughout a situation.

In I Corinthians, Paul deals with one of the most controversial subjects in Christiandom, the sign gifts, the gifts of knowledge, prophecy, and tongues. God's preference is for us to have clear understanding of truth, thus Paul gives three critical pieces of truth concerning tongues.

1. **The Biblical Position of Tongues**. The word prophecy means speaking plainly to people. Prophecy, in the first century, was the ability the Holy Spirit gave preachers to speak the Word of God with special insights; as they were teaching or preaching and God giving them truths on the spot. On the other hand, prophecy today is different. Preachers have to study and pray, asking God for understanding of the Scriptures. Paul gives a three-fold purpose for prophecy: *First*, prophecy edifies the entire Church, however, tongues only edify the speaker. He says, "...howbeit in the Spirit he speaketh mysteries, but he that prophesieth, speaketh plainly, and speaketh unto men, to build up, edification, exaltation and comfort. He that speaketh in a tongue edifieth himself, the speaker" (I Cor. 14:2-5). *Second*, prophecy exempts people. In I Cor. 14:6-12, Paul introduces the subject of understanding. The parable of the sower and the seed teaches us that Satan's objective is to snatch the Word so that we don't understand it. When we don't understand it, it cannot benefit us. So Paul is saying, there is a need for understanding the Word of God. Not only does prophecy edify, but tongues brings about a perplexity that exempts us from understanding and applying the Word to our lives. *Third*, tongue speaking should never be practiced before the unsaved. The unsaved need the Gospel of Jesus Christ. The speaking gifts are for preaching truth!

2. **The Biblical Procedure for Tongues**. Paul instructs the church that no more than three people are allowed to speak in a tongue, and if they speak, let there be an interpreter. If there is no interpreter, keep quiet. This policy is a regulation that God

has laid down in His Word (I Cor. 14:28). Satan has divided the body of Christ with misunderstandings and debates over this issue. As believers, it is more important to get people saved than to worry about who believes in tongues. We tend to major in the minors and minor in the majors. We are to come together in the Name of Jesus, one Lord, one faith, one baptism.

3. **The Biblical Preference for the Church.** In I Cor. 14:28-38, new revelation has precedence over the new proclamation. We have taken experience over exposition. We must speak plainly to people, knowing that order dispels dysfunction, division, and order is decent and divine. If you are confused, call on Jesus and let Him lead you to speak when the Spirit specifies.

Still Standing

In spite of all Satan's attacks, deceptions, and all his weaponry, we are still standing. If ever there were promises by God of protection, of power over pitfalls, and of victory over the devil's venom, it is Jesus' declaration in Matthew 16:18. He promises the future church, in spite of the warfare, there will still be worship; in spite of satanic oppositions, there will still be order; and in spite of demonic difficulty, there will still be divine deliverance. We are not keeping ourselves; we are being kept by the power of Almighty God. We are kept from falling away from the faith because the gates of Hell will not prevail against the Church. We must remember that Christ is Lord of the program called The Church. Thus, there are four critical aspects of the Church:

1. **The Transition of the Church by Christ.** In Matthew 16:18, Jesus says that upon this rock (the rock of Christ), I will build My Church. Jesus is speaking futuristically of the Church Age. We are currently in the Church Age. And in spite of our weariness, wounds, and even Satan's wickedness, the gates (the powers and authority) of Hell shall not prevail against the Church. This is because Christ builds His Church upon Himself. There is a major transition from God's program with Israel to the program of the Church.

2. **The Translation of the Church by Christ.** In Acts 1:4, we are told that after Christ arose, He told His followers to wait for the promise of the Father, the baptism of the Holy Spirit with fire. Jesus would not tell them the time of His return (we are not to know the time). He also promised them power when the Holy Spirit would come upon them. Telling them that they would become witnesses for Christ in Jerusalem, Judea, Samaria and to the uttermost parts of the earth. The new program of the Church says that they, and consequently we, are not staying in Jerusalem. We will go to Germany, Russia, Spain, etc. The purpose for Christ's translation is so that He may send the Holy Spirit. The Spirit will abide, lead, guide, protect, teach, equip, empower, and enable us to be victorious. *The promise is that the Holy Spirit will be a permanent presence of God on the inside.* The picture from the Old Testament is of the smitten rock in the wilderness. This rock, when it was smitten, produced water. When Jesus died (was smitten on the cross), the free flow of the Holy Spirit could be introduced to us, but Jesus had to be transported into Heaven first.

3. **The Transference of the Church through Christ**. At Pentecost, Christ transfers His ministry to the Holy Spirit. When the Spirit came, there was a rushing mighty wind that filled the whole house where the followers of Christ were and cloven tongues like fire sat on each of them (Acts 2:2). They spoke in tongues, which is not ecstatic speech. The word "tongues" means languages. Jews from every nation heard the gospel in their own language. Through this transference, the Holy Spirit becomes the superintendent of the Church Age, and the gates of Hell shall not prevail against the Church.

4. **The Triumph of the Church with Christ.** 2 Corinthians 4:1 tells us that we have this ministry therefore, we faint not. There is a power base which keeps us going when we feel like quitting. We experience problems, but He gives us power (V.6). We are like trash, but we have a treasure that the power may be of God, and not of us (V.7). We are troubled, but have the triumph. We are chased, but we are never crushed (V.8). Our pain (this light affliction) is temporary, but our profit is permanent (V.17). Our feelings are transformed into faith (V.18). Our hope is in heaven. The gates of Hell shall not permanently wound us, not control us, not confound us, not wear us out, and not win against us. Victory is ours! The gates of Hell shall not prevail against us. Therefore, we are still standing!

PROPHECY

Blessed is he that readeth, and they that hear the words of this prophecy, and keep those things which are written therein: for the time is at hand.

Revelation 1:3

The Purpose for My Patmos

If there are any questions about Jesus Christ, they are answered in the book of Revelation, chapter one. Jesus is Potentate, King of kings, Lord of lords, and the Majestic One of the universe. Under the influence of the Holy Spirit, John wrote the book, conveying Jesus as Savior and Lord. John received from God information that would dramatically change his attitude about Jesus. In John chapter 17, the Apostle saw Jesus: However, in the Revelation, John portrays Jesus not as a Lamb, but as a Lion, not only as Savior, but as Sovereign.

John was in his nineties and the last living Apostle when the Roman Emperor Dominion ruled. At the time, there was heavy persecution, and many were killed just because they named the Name of Jesus Christ. John explained to the Church of that day that he was a companion in their suffering (V.9). Because John; (1) preached the Word of God, and (2) testified of the Lord Jesus Christ, he was banished to the isle of Patmos.

Sometimes God cannot speak to us where we are, so He creates situations. He spoke to Moses in the wilderness, Paul in the third Heaven, Daniel in captivity, Jonah in the belly of a great fish. "Go to the potter's house and there I'll give you a word ..." Jer. 18:12. Therefore, on the Lord's Day, John was caught up in a vision, and was delivered from Patmos to Heaven.

Once in heaven, John heard a great voice as of a trumpet behind him saying, "I am Alpha and Omega, the first and the last" (V.11a). Jesus identified Himself, and gave John instructions about what to write, (since He is the Word), and where to send the book the seven churches in Asia. John not only heard the Voice of the Lord, he also had a vision of the Lord. In his vision, the emphasis was light. Symbolic language was used there because it is one thing to hear God's voice, but it is quite another to see Him. **We see Him when we find out who He is** (metaphorically). John saw Jesus symbolically dressed as Judge and King (V.13). In verse 14 John saw Jesus with white hair, as white as snow (pure and eternal), and His eyes were a flame of fire (showing His anger with the church and the world system). During his vision John saw Jesus in the midst of the lamp stand. This symbolized that the Lord Jesus Christ is the center of attraction in Heaven and Earth. If He's not the center of attraction, He won't be in the midst. Jesus refuses to accept second place. He must be number one on the priority list. In John 17:5, Jesus asked the Father to give Him back His Glory, which He had with Him before the world. In the light of His Glory all must fall on their knees in obedience to his Lordship, in awe and fear. God sends help when it looks the darkest. He sends His light, the Lord Jesus Christ. John wrote, "When I saw Him I fell at His feet as dead" (V.17a). However, Jesus, who is all powerful and will judge the quick and the dead, comforted John and said, "Fear not, I am the first and the last; I am He that liveth, and was dead; and behold, I am alive for evermore, Amen; and have the keys of hell and death" (vv.17-18). It will cost us to name the Name of Jesus in the last days.

But, thanks be to God we have the Victory through the Name of the Lord Christ Jesus!

Beauty and the Beast

The greatest satanic assault on mankind is the final assault of the anti-Christ which enslaves the world with a wickedness never before seen by man. When the anti-Christ comes, the Holy Spirit will move out and let evil take over. It is a horrific, horrendous and horrible last stand for Satan. This is what Daniel talked about; the abomination of desolation, the seventh week of Daniel, the time of Jacob's trouble, the 666, the great tribulation, it is here that man is in deep, dark trouble.

The church needs to tell friends, family neighbors and enemies that they need to get saved. This is not a time to play around. The church will not be here when the Holy Spirit raptures the church. The world will not know that the church has left. Life will go on as usual. They will come up with some tremendous story about what happened to millions of people vanishing all at once. The book of the Revelation and Daniel fit like hand and glove. You cannot interpret one without the other. Both are prophecy of the great last days.

Daniel was privileged by God to receive a video of the venomous master. It is in this context that, Daniel Chaps. 7 and 8 lays out for us Beauty, which is the Lord Jesus Christ, and the beast, who is the anti-Christ. Everything that is happening is a clear indicator that the rapture is near. The Middle East events will become worst, and all events in the Middle East are indicators of where we are chronologically according to the Word of God.

1. **The Definition of the Beast** (Daniel 7:1-7). Daniel did not understand the image that was being shown to him. Daniel was fearful because he saw a little horn, not knowing that the little horn is the Anti-Christ. The ten toes are symbolic of a ten nation confederacy that will take place at the time of the tribulation. The Little horn will rise up under the revised Roman Empire, and he will conquer three of the ten nations and take over the world and be energized by the devil.

2. **The Devastation of the Beast** (Daniel 7:8). The anti-Christ will come into power with these two systems; religion and politics. We, as a church, should not become caught up in the climate of politics and world religions. In Revelation Chap. 6, we will see judgments that are coming down from Heaven to earth. These are not bad beasts, they are the four living creatures that are around the throne of God. Then, in comes four horses;

one white with a bow. This is not Christ. This is the anti-Christ because Jesus does not carry a bow, He carries a sword. Another came in with red, which is bloodshed. The third horse, black, brought famine, and the fourth horse, pale, brought death. God is going to give Satan the key to open up Tarterus, where the fallen angels (Genesis 6) were locked away by God. They are going to kill one-third of mankind. Satan's time is real short. Anyone who does not believe Jesus Christ was crucified is part of a false religious system. Satan will devastate the earth. He will make people think that he has world peace, but it will be a false peace.

3. **The Defeat of the Beast** (Daniel 7:9-18). God has the last word. Jesus has the key that determines everything. He is your Redeemer. He is in control. He has a timetable for all things. Satan has some power, but God has all power. He came as a Lamb, but He is coming back as a Lion. The 144,000 Jews will not be witnessing the Gospel of grace, but the Gospel of the Kingdom. They will be telling people about salvation and that Jesus is King. Jesus is coming and will defeat all with the Word of God. He will take the anti-Christ and the False Prophet into the lake of fire forever. He will then call the strong angels down out of heaven with chains to wrap them around Satan and lock him up for a thousand years. Jesus is going to rule with a rod of iron.

He is King of kings and Lord of lords, and the Church will be with Him. God will put Satan into the Lake of Fire. Next, the Great White throne of Judgment will take place. There will be a new Heaven, and new earth. There will be no more crying, dying or pain. The Lord has conquered the beast. The Lamb has died for all our sins. God who is rich in mercy has saved us. It is Jesus the Christ. Praise Him for He is worthy to be praised!

The Final Assault

There has been a cosmic war from the beginning of time that will determine which kingdom will be left standing. The raging of this battle is between light and darkness, good and evil. The conflict began when Lucifer took one third of the angels and tried to overthrow Almighty God (Isaiah 14). Satan has influenced the world system since his fall. Now we are looking into the face of the coming final assault.

The final assault can be seen in a five-fold manner:

1. **The Meeting**: Revelation 4 is the beginning of this final assault. The rapture occurs and the tribulation is immediately ushered in. God the Father is on the throne (Rev. 4:2). Around the throne is a rainbow, 24 elders who represent the Church and four living creatures that depict the creation and wisdom of God. Out from the throne are storm signals of coming judgment. There will be worship to the One on the throne (vv.8,11). What a meeting!

2. **The Marriage and the Mystery**: In Revelation 5 we see a scroll with seven seals. It is the title deed to the universe that only Jesus can unlock. Every seal is a judgment on earth. No one is worthy to open the seals but Jesus. Innumerable angels sing, "Worthy is the Lamb." The most important thing we can do with our lives is to worship Jesus Christ.

3. **The Madness**: Revelation 6 begins the description of the Tribulation period. The Church is gone. There is a false prince who makes a covenant with Israel to protect them (Dan. 9). Then he will turn on them. There will be a remnant of innumerable Gentiles, (not the Church), who will be martyred. In Revelation 7 we are told of the redeemed Jews (vv.1-8) and Gentiles (vv.9-17), who come out of the Tribulation. In Revelation 8, a seal is opened that causes silence in Heaven for half an hour because something is ready to break out. The earth, seas, rivers, heavens, and mankind will be afflicted with judgment. There will be a strong delusion to believe the lie. In Revelation 9 all the demonic forces will be let out of Hell. They are like scorpions which afflict mankind. From chapters 10 to 14 is the middle of the Tribulation. The Satanic trio (Satan, anti-Christ, and the false prophet) will come to the front. Chapter 11 introduces the two witnesses who preach and call down fire. Then the anti-Christ wipes them out on the street, but three days later

God raises them up. Satan is relegated to the earth in chapter 12. He will have no more jurisdictions to the throne of God. In chapters 17 and 18 there is the last victory over the beast (the religious and political systems) on which the antiChrist rides. The religious system (Rev. 17), is called Jezebel because the system deviates from the Gospel of Christ. What should the Church watch for? Look for politics to come into the church. Look for religious values and positions that are not Biblical to emerge.

4. **The Mandate:**   Jesus returns to earth with the saints and angelic hosts to fight the battle of Armageddon (Rev. 19). Satan is bound for a thousand years (Rev. 20). The Millennial Kingdom is set up and all the promises in Isaiah are in affect. Then God will let Satan out for a time followed by the Great White Throne Judgment. There will be a judge, but no jury; a prosecution, but no defense; a sentence, but no appeal.

5. **The Magnificence:**   In Revelation chapters 21 and 22 there is a new Heaven and a earth. It is the land of NO MORE, for there will be no more curse, death, tears, or pain. A new Heaven will come down made of precious gems with the throne of God in the middle. This is where we will be in glory.

We are living in this age under Satanic influence. Satan wants us to be neutral, to stop believing what the Word of God says, but God has a plan for His people. Therefore, be steadfast, hold on, stand still, and wait on Jesus. When we are steadfast God has our back!

God's Divine Explosion

God's Holy City was subdued. Jerusalem, that city of peace, had forfeited her name. The city had witnessed an evil murder of the Promised Messiah. God the Father had orchestrated every event to fall in line with His Eternal Plan. God chose every actor and actress to participate in this arrangement. However, now the play had come to an intermission, and a solemn quietness loomed over the city.

The disciples had fled and lost hope. Some had acknowledged guilt. The religious leaders had committed the unpardonable sin, even the <u>universe</u> had rebelled against the temperature in Jerusalem. The sun went on strike and stopped shining. The moon started hemorrhaging. The earth started railing and rocking. All was quiet, the Messiah was truly dead. A guard was posted at a borrowed tomb. Suddenly, there was an enormous <u>explosion</u>, a detonation, and a sudden release.

God had spiritually wired a divine bomb to explode at a precise period in time. This detonation consisted of something which can be called Hypo 52 – Hypostatic Union. The union of two explosives – 100% perfect man and 100% perfect God. This combination, in turn, triggered three separate explosions.

1. **The Explosion of His Predictions** (Explanations - Luke 24:6-8). God had prophesied in Gen. 3:15, that His heel would be bruised,. When a heel is bruised, it affects our ability to stand. He had to fall (die), but the word "bruise" is a term for temporary inactivity. The Word goes on to say that, "He would crush His head" (a death blow).

In Psalms 16, the psalmist wrote, "Thou wilt not leave my soul in Hell, neither wilt thou suffer thine Holy One to see corruption," (no decomposition). In Psalms 118, the psalmist stated, "The stone which the builders refused is become the head stone of the corner." Isaiah 53:5 says, "He was <u>wounded</u> for our transgression. He was <u>bruised</u> for our iniquities, the chastisement of our peace was upon Him, and with His stripes we are healed."

God also furnished prophecy and predictions of:

- (a) Two Birds
- (b) A Known Redeemer
- (c) Two Priesthoods
- (d) Two Trees

The Explosion of His <u>Predictions</u> was overwhelming explanations, which were given **beforehand.**

2. **The Explosions of His Power**

- (a) An Earthquake by definition is a shaking or trembling of the earth caused by underground forces or by breaking and shifting of rock beneath the surface. The earthquake was the force of Him being the Rock of God. Not only was there the earthquake, but there was an unusual <u>Evidence</u>.
- (b) The Grave Clothes

3. **The Explosion of His Provision**

Election, Predestination, Sanctification, Glorification, Salvation, Satisfaction – Peace

O.T. Saints were Led Out
N.T. Saints were Snatched Out

Insight Produces Foresight

One of the greatest gifts given to the Believer is the level of insight and wisdom that God affords His people. God gives us a perspective on the past, providence on the present, and a prescription for the future. Daniel Chapter 9 shows an unfolding of His plan and prophesies concerning His people. God has secrets. There is the Revealed Will of God; The Word, the Permissive Will of God; what He allows, and the Secret Will of God; only what He knows. Too often we become confused with these actions of God. We will never know the Secret Will of God.

Through the Revealed Word of God, we can have peace, power, and prosperity. Today, we do not want the Revealed Word of God. We pretend that we know the Secret Will of God. He has not revealed these secrets. There are things that have happened in our lives that we had no way of knowing. There will be in our future paths, things that we will never anticipate because only God knows these secrets.

Daniel has many concerns about things that are about to transpire. This chapter will help us to see how God speaks through His Word, and we speak to Him through prayer. There is no more revelation; God is not giving us new messages. All scripture is for our information, but not for our participation. We cannot open the Word of God, claim a promise, and apply it to our lives. That is characteristic of a false premise of the last days.

1. **Daniel has a Comprehension of God's Plan** (vv.1-2). God did not give Daniel a vision. He gave him the Word. God is not giving us a vision; He has given us His Word. If we want to know Jesus, follow the Word. We must not believe in visions, feelings or experiences. Thy Word have I hidden in my heart, that I may not sin against thee. We must rightly divide the Word. The Old Testament is the New Testament revealed; the New Testament is the Old Testament concealed. All scripture is God breathed. People are perishing for a lack of knowledge. If God is speaking to you, it should be verified in the Word.

2. **Daniel's Confession of God's Precept** (vv.3-19). Daniel recognizes and prays for the sins of the nation. He added himself to what his forefathers did. Daniel is praying for the city, the sanctuary, and for the people. He prays in response to God's Word, with fervency, an attitude of self-denial, dependence for God's character, the goal of God's glory, and he is strengthened with confession. As we pray, we all should; confess, repent, praise,

and give thanks. In the midst of Daniel's confession God sent restoration.

3. **Daniel Calculates God's Prophesy** (vv.20-27) God did a calculation; 69 weeks and the Messiah will be cut off. There will then be a divine time out. God will bring in the Church. Only He will know how long the Church Age will last and when the Church is caught up. The Jews will have only one more week, seven years, to fulfill the seventh week of Daniel. The anti-Christ will pretend to be the protector, but Jesus will kill the anti-Christ, kill the False Prophet, and put Satan in the lake of fire. Then there will be a new Heaven and earth. God showed Daniel everything concerning His people.

God specializes in a timetable that only He knows. Daniel, Abraham, nor Peter could interpret it. Daniel did not understand the Church Age. God also specializes in time-out of our resources, trials, and tribulations. Every time we get into trouble God will call a time-out and usher something back in. Daniel had comprehension, confession, and calculation because he blessed God, and God gave him a video of the future.

There are some secret things that God will do for us too. When we want to give up God will show up. We serve a God who is in control. God keeps giving us the victory. He is able to prepare a table in the presence of our enemies. He is awesome, and He knows what we need even before we ask. We must learn how to transfer our troubles, so we can become triumphant. God knows when to restore and rebuild us. We should praise Him, because Jesus is the Christ, the Son of the Living God. Praise Him!

Ready or Not, Here I Come

Eternal life is the most precious promise given to every believer. It has a quantitative as well as a qualitative aspect. It depicts another realm of existence to which we can look forward. A panoramic view of the Bible enables one to see the prologue of life in Genesis, which is time, and the epilogue in Revelation, which is eternity.

The Book of the Revelation provides us with a preview of the things to come. *We will be with God, like God and ever learning more about God.* The concluding chapter extends an invitation to a new place, provides motivation for praise, and inspiration for new peace. John includes a set of instructions for worship, wisdom, and it contains a warning. God instructed John to disclose the truth.

John opens this final chapter with an invitation to a new place for a new people. This is an invitation to the citizens of the city (vv.1-6). What makes heaven so great is that we will dwell with God. There are several emblems used to describe what it will be like. The pure river represents salvation and life. This life is a different kind of life. It is a river that flows straight from the throne of God. It represents the abundant life. The tree described, bears fruit perpetually. Its leaves provide healing and remove the curse. In this new place our service will be new and perfected. We will wear his name on our foreheads as identification. It is an invitation to reign with Him forever. Every believer has an ultimate desire to be like God. Even as we look forward to what will be, confirmation that this invitation has been extended to us, is our desire to be like Him.

We are motivated to praise the living God because of the prophecy, the power, and the Person of Christ. He will come quickly. John was instructed not to seal the prophecy, nor worship the angel, who is just a messenger of God; instead, he must worship God. The parameters were described . . . "Let He that is unjust, be unjust still . . . and he that is holy, let him be holy still" (V.11). The power of the Lord motivates us to praise Him, as He will come quickly and give to every man according to his work (V.12). Finally, we are motivated to praise Him because of the person of Christ. He is the Alpha and the Omega, the beginning and the end, the first and the last. He is the root and the offspring of David. We praise him for being the bright and morning star. We are motivated to praise and inspired by a promise of peace.

"And the Spirit and the bride say come . . . And let him that is athirst come. And whosoever will, let him take of the water of life freely." Oh to be with Him, and to be like Him, and to access Him freely.

We are invited, motivated, and inspired. *The great news is while we look forward to all these things, we have available to us a foretaste of the abundant life.* **He has come to give us life that we should have it more abundantly**. He also has granted us access to come boldly before the throne of grace to receive mercy and grace to help in our time of need. We should be motivated and inspired to praise and serve Him now!

Time is Running Out

One of the darkest deceptions known to mankind is the emergence of the anti-Christ. He is the disciple of delusion, epitomizing evil. He is referred to as the man of sin and lawlessness. Influencing, infecting and inflaming the entire world, he is an evil being with great power. He will launch an open rebellion against Christ. Revelation calls him the beast. Matthew calls him the false Christ. Empowered by the devil, his number is 666. The anti-Christ is the troublemaker during the  Tribulation period. He will not be exposed until the Church has been raptured out. Understanding this, John begins to warn the Church about the reality of the antichrist. John is revealing that God has a plan.

The anti-Christ can be analyzed and understood from several dimensions. First there is the spirit of anti-Christ. This spirit is anything religious, social or otherwise that opposes Jesus Christ. It has been active since the time of Genesis chapter 3. Anything that opposes the deity of Christ is part of the anti-Christ. The spirit of anti-Christ will be replaced with the person."Little children, it is the last time: as ye have heard that antichrist shall come" (I John 2:18). John lays out the age, the arrival of the anti-Christ, and the affirmation for Believers.

John speaks of the last hour. It is the last hour since the ascension of Christ. Time is running out. We can look at the condition of the world and sin within it and determine that the age is upon us. God is about to do His thing. Aren't you glad God didn't come back before you accepted Jesus Christ? Right now the Holy Ghost is restraining evil while the Church remains and God's program is being completed; but time is running out. The Spirit of anti-Christ is prevalent.

There are three things that characterize someone who is dominated by the spirit of anti-Christ. First, they depart from the fellowship. "They went out from us, but they were not of us" (V.19). These people have a form of godliness, but deny the power. God's people enjoy being around each other. "Saved people have unction from the Holy Ghost" (V.20). We have a special knowledge of God and from God. Secondly, "those under the influence of the spirit of antichrist deny the faith" (vv.21-25). "Who is a liar but he that denieth that Jesus is the Christ? He is antichrist, that denieth the Father and the Son" (V.22). What you believe about Jesus answers it all. Outside of Christ, there is no relationship or access to God the Father. Finally, those who have the spirit of anti-Christ try to deceive the faithful by seducing us to believe a lie. "These things have I written unto you concerning them that seduce you" (V.26). Satan has a counterfeit gospel, counterfeit ministers, and a counterfeit program. Don't believe the lie!

Those dominated by the spirit of anti-Christ depart from the fellowship, deny the faith, and try to deceive the faithful. John lays out three affirmations for those who are saved. First, we must abide in Christ. We are to remain in Him. We ought to believe and anticipate His appearing. Finally, "as we abide and anticipate His appearing we will not be ashamed when He comes" (V.28).

Time is running out. Are you ready? Are you abiding and anticipating?

When the Hand Writing Is On the Wall

The majesty of God is always designed to make a statement about His Person, His people, and His purposes. These statements deal with His mastery over the universe, His Lordship over both the angelic and demonic realms of existence, and His light over darkness. God is able to silence the sinister of sin, break the backs of boasting men, and derail the deceived. In the context of Daniel chapter 5, we will see a (6) step process of God, 5 of which will annul and punish the wicked. It is here that a party 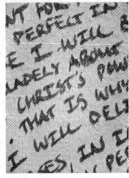 was turned into a punishment, drunks are driven to soberness, hell rousers are humbled, and boasters are brought back to God beckoning call.

We will also learn that God hates pride and pollution. God is for His purposes and His people. When people decide to ignore the Holy Spirit, do their own thing, and think there will be no recourse; God shows up with Handwriting on the wall. We are being judged right now for our faithfulness with using our gifts, giving, and giving Him Glory. It is here that we will see why God had Daniel in captivity for seventy years. There is a message here for the saved and the unsaved. God is not to be played with, He is in control at all times. He has a way to bring light to darkness, and righteousness to unrighteousness.

1. **There is a Demonic Hall** (Negative - Dan. 5:1). While a party was going on in the palace; the Medes and the Persians were attacking. This was a wrong time to attack the ball. This ball was demonic because it was a denunciation of the righteousness of God. Some of us are so blind that we too decide to do something against God at the wrong time. We need to be careful how we live, talk, and walk. None of us are perfect, but we will give an account for deliberate sin.

2. **There is a Deceived Fall** (Nerve - Dan. 5:2). There is a deception of self and a total disrespect for God. Belshazzar ignored God. He disrespected His Holiness, and the Power and the Glory of Almighty God. He became drunk, called for sanctified vessels, and drank wine from these vessels, which were now attributed to the gods of Babylon. When we take a sanctified situation and turn it into dirt, expect some hand writing to go on the wall. We cannot go back to the vomit that Jesus has sanctified us from.

3. **There is a Divine Wall** (Notice - Dan. 5:3-6). In the midst of the party they saw fingers moving on the wall. This wall was divine, because God was writing on it. Whenever God writes with His finger, it is either for a word, wisdom, or a warning. At Mt. Sinai, Exodus 19-20, God wrote the commandments on the wall of the mountain. In John chapter 9, Jesus wrote on the ground with His finger. He has allowed some strange things through out the Bible.

4. **There is a Depressing Crawl** (Note - Dan. 5:23-28). Method, Meaning, and Movement. This scrawl was his doom. God is not mocked. Some people have to learn the hard way. When will you learn your lesson? What blinds us from the will and word of God? It is called SIN. If God wrote your life out today, could you receive it with Joy?

5. **There is a Devastative Awe** (Nose Dive - Dan. 5:30-31). God gave Israel favor with Darius. When we are obedient with God, He opens doors that no man can open. Please God and Praise Him, because He is able to bless our table. He will give us joy in the midst of your trouble.

But God, pulled us out with a call, He is rich in mercy. Paul said we were dead in trespasses and sin, But God! If it had not been for the Lord, who was on our side. But God! It was only God that put us on the street called straight. But God! It was God that clothed us. But God! It was God that ordered us steps. But God! It was God that can change our heart. But God! It is God that can change our walk. But God! He will become our joy. He is an awesome God. The call called us out of hell. It was Jesus that called us. Thank God for the call. Praise the name of Jesus.

Where Do We Go From Here?

There's no greater joy, than when an individual who was tired and worn, goes on vacation. In capsule form, it is a therapeutic breaking away from problems, people and performances. It allows one to reap, recover, and reassess. The only shortcoming that a vacation seems to have is that it always seems to end too soon.

Much the same way, as we live our daily lives. We too are confronted with problems, people and performances, and what seems to be therapeutic for the child of God is that we will go on a permanent vacation, one day. We will break away from this sin-cursed world and travel to what has been described as a haven of joy. I believe that our knowledge and beliefs regarding where we are going after death, dictate how we live and what we do, while on Earth. Undoubtedly, there has been much speculation on the hereafter. Some believe in reincarnation; that is after death, we return in another form. Some have taught the unbelievable doctrine of soul-sleep, which says that when you die, you sleep in the grave.

However, the Bible has two things to say about two different groups of people, who are going to two different places. The Bible says that the unsaved, when they die, will face judgment; they go to an intermediate state called "Hell," where they will await their eternal state, which is The Lake of Fire.

For those who are saved, the Bible says, "To be absent from the body is to be present with the Lord." Both of those statements point to two different places. To say this in simplistic form: For those who are born twice, they only die once. But the real question is: "Where do we go from here?" The Bible is clear on where both the saved and the unsaved will go.

1. **The Promise**
     A. A promise of a place that has been prepared (vv.1,2)
     B. A promise of a package designed for God's people (v.3)

2. **The Picture**
     A. There are two graphic pictures of Heaven (II Cor.12) Paul had been caught up at Lystra.
     B. Acts 14 – He died and apparently was caught up to Heaven. This dialogue is picked up in II Corinthians, as Paul is speaking in second person.
     C. Revelation 1:9 – John the Apostle – who had been exiled on the Isle of Patius.

3. **The Place**

    A. The descent of the city (Rev. 21:1, 2)

    B. The description of the city (Rev. 21:3-22, 25)

    C. The delegates (occupants) of this city – The Father, the Son & the Holy Spirit; The Holy and Elect Angels; the 24 elders; the Church and all of the Redeemed

    D. The location – The New Jerusalem is pictured as a stationary city floating above the earth in space. The new earth will become a satellite planet encircling the starry capital from which the earth will review its light.

    E. The size – 1500 square miles (NYC to Denver, CO – from Canada to Florida)

    F. The shape – like a cube (some say pyramid)

    G. The gates – 12 gates, made of pearls

    H. The foundations – made of diamonds, sapphires, rubies, jasper stars (4)

    I. The street – pure transparent gold

    J. The activities – Heaven will be a place of learning

For we know, in part, that Heaven will be a place of fellowship. As we think about Heaven, let's ask ourselves, what will we experience the first five minutes after death – before the funeral?

- ☐ Our first experience will be that death was so easy; it was like falling to sleep and waking up in a beautiful world. There was no valley of death, no demons, no dark river to cross – that a ministering angel was waiting to convoy us to Paradise (as they carried Lazarus – Luke 16). What a delight to meet our Guardian angel who watched over us in our earthly life.

- ☐ We leave behind our earthly bodies, with all of its weaknesses, sufferings, and limitations; and we have a spiritual body suited for Heaven.

- ☐ Our third experience will be that we are being transported swiftly through space toward a beautiful century, where radiance is brighter than the sun. As we approach Heaven, groups of angels will come out to escort us home – singing, "Blessed are they that do His commandment, that they might have a right to the Tree of Life, and enter into the gates of His city."

- ☐ We will find a totally new atmosphere of love; there will be no discord or sin.

☐   We will see and feel near to Jesus.

☐   We will meet all of the Saints that have gone before us .

Yes, we will experience the Promise, we will have a Picture, we will see the Place, but finally we will be united with the Praise!

You Can't Battle the Books

Sentencing for a felon, who has been found guilty by jury, does not take place at the time of the verdict. Instead, the presiding Judge sets a future date for sentencing. On that appointed date, the court reconvenes for sentencing. Typically, the Judge will recap the jury's finding and give the defendant an opportunity to address the court prior to rendering the sentence. Once the sentence has been read, immediately the defendant is hurried out of the courtroom to begin serving his sentence.

Spiritually, the day of sentencing takes place in the Book of the Revelation, chapter 20. It is the day of reckoning. Everyone was found guilty in the Book of Romans. All have sinned and come short of the glory of God. There is none righteous. In fact, there are 14 indictments against man listed in Romans. Man's guilt goes back to the Garden of Eden with Adam and Eve. In Revelation, God is reconvening the court to administer the sentence.

There is a great deal of confusion about Judgment Day. Believers have already been judged at the cross. His death was our death. His resurrection was our resurrection. Having been found guilty, but now declared righteous, we are seated in heavenly places because we are in Christ. God imputed Christ's righteousness to us and imparted His Spirit in us. Thanks be to God!

Leading up to the day of reckoning, in Revelation chapter 4, the church is raptured, chapter 5 is the Glorification of the Lamb, chapters 6 through 19 is the Tribulation period, chapter 20 brings us to the Great White Throne Judgment. The picture of the Day of Reckoning is painted with a chain, a claim, the reign, the blame, and finally, the shame. A study of this chapter makes it apparent that God has a plan for the ages.

"And I saw an angel come down from heaven having the key of the bottomless pit and a great chain in his hand" (Rev 20: 1). Judgment begins with Satan being chained and tossed into the bottomless pit. He is bound in the pit for 1,000 years. Too many people have a misconception that God and Satan are in a spiritual battle to determine whether good or evil shall prevail. God is in control of Satan. God controls, conquers and cancels evil. The angel shows up to let Satan know that his time is up. He is put under restraint. The chain is followed by the claim of the Old Testament and tribulation saints.

"And I saw the thrones. and I saw the souls of them that were beheaded for the witness of Christ" (Rev. 20:4). The claim is the resurrection of the Old Testament saints and those Believers who lost their lives during the Tribulation period. We who have been saved during the Church Age have already been raptured out. After the first resurrection, Christ sets up His reign.

The earthly reign of Christ will last for 1,000 years. This is His Millennium Reign (Rev 20: 6). Christ will reign with an iron rod. This is the time spoken of in Isaiah. The curse of the earth will be removed. Lion and lamb will lie down together. Although there is harmony, salvation will not necessarily be available. God will prove that with a perfect environment, perfect education, and perfect employment, man will still be evil. Why? Because he is evil by nature. At the end of the reign of Christ, Satan gets the blame.

Satan is loosed out of prison and shall go out to deceive the nations (Rev. 20: 7-8). The blame comes when he is cast into the lake of fire and brimstone. He joins the beast and the false prophet and is tormented day and night forever and ever (Rev. 20: 10). The shame of all unbelievers follows the blame.

I saw the dead, small and great stand before God; and the books were opened (Rev. 20:12). This is the unbelievers reckoning. The Books contain all their works, which will be judged. Every violation of their conscious, tongue, public works, and secret works will be judged. Since the blood of the Lord Jesus Christ has not covered their sins, they must be judged for their works. All that was done in secret shall be revealed. And another book was opened which is the book of life. And whosoever was not found written in the book of life was cast into the lake of fire. (Rev. 20:13,15).

Thank God for such a great salvation! Just when the Believer is about to be judged, our Attorney, Advocate, Kinsmen Redeemer shows up with the nail prints in His hand. Our sentence is thrown out and we are declared righteous. We have been redeemed!

Preparation

LORD, thou hast heard the desire of the humble: thou wilt prepare their heart, thou wilt cause thine ear to hear.

Psalm 10:17

Commitment is the glue for glorifying God. As we commit to perseverance through our problems, we in turn are blessed with an unusual contentment. However, there is a greater blessing for those who are able to commit and compromise through times of trouble, conflict, and confusion. It is then that God performs a powerful platform of peace and spiritual prosperity within us. Can you love and give to those that won't give back to you? Most of us stay in our egocentric circles as long as our lives are okay. Get out of the "me" syndrome. When we can leave our comfort zones and move out into the conflict areas of life and reach, teach, disciple, and help people for Jesus Christ, then that is true ministry. Joshua was deceived by people who came back only to discover they needed him. Watch what you say and do to others, you may need them sooner than you think. The hole that you dig for others, you may fall into it yourself. Joshua made a bad decision, and in his decision making, God held him to his word. Notice God's response to Joshua's responsibilities.

1. **God Ordered a New Difficulty** (vv.1-7). He orders these for our growth and dependency on Him. James 1:2-4, ". . . count it all joy when you fall into divers' temptation . . ." God tested Joshua's commitment. The logic of the battle was that all nations are upset with Gibeon because they made an alliance with Israel. Gibeon was a choice tribe with the best fighting men. Satan watches alliances and he will not allow you to align yourselves with one another against him. Just when you feel joyful, have victory; something will come to devastate you. In reading Job chapter 2, what we do not always realize is that God is behind the scenes ordering difficulty. The purpose is to strengthen us and to change our perspective; His Person and our problems.

2. **God Ordered a New Dedication** (vv.8-10). It is not until we get in trouble that we realize it is God who orders our victory. Joshua's power, position, and pity came from God. He was more sympathetic to the Gibeonites than anyone else. The people who have deceived you may come back into your lives and you need to receive them. Stop holding others hostage. God is challenging Joshua to a new level of dedication.

3. **God Ordered a New Destruction** (vv.11-40). God ordered Joshua into battle and more soldiers were killed because of the storm rather than Joshua's sword. When God asks you to do

something, He has already completed it. As Joshua prayed, God made the sun stand still. He is able to make things happen that you will never be able to figure out. The Lord fought for Israel.

4. **God Ordered a New Defense** (vv.41-42). The only way we will have power and peace is to have Jesus fight for us. Joshua won the battle because God fought for him. He is the author and finisher of our faith. He is the prescription for victory. Jesus is in control when we get out of control.

He is an on-time God. "But they that wait upon the Lord shall renew their Strength; they shall mount up with wings as eagles; they shall run, and not be weary; and they shall walk, and not faint." If confused or in conflict, we must be still and let Jesus lead us. There are no alternatives. Know that He is God. He is able!

Are You Ready to Depart?

There is an association between deliverance, departure and direction in the life of the Believer. Deliverance comes when we depart from our old way of thinking. Our direction is received from the Word of God. We must depart from our dependencies. Our departing should not be done looking back, as did Lot's wife; instead, it should be done looking forward with purpose, profit, passion and praise.

In the closing of II Timothy, Paul provides an example of how we ought to depart. He is not bothered or bitter about his departure. He is brave. Although he is about to have his head cut off, he still has the mind of Christ. Paul's perspective is right. When trouble comes, we need the peace of God which comes from practicing the presence of God. Paul's closing statements represent the perfect dialogue for dying. What is God challenging you to depart from? When God calls us from one thing He calls us into another.

Paul's departing dialogue indicates it was time for three things: a time of realization, a time of reflection, and a time of release. "For I am now ready to be offered, and the time of my departure is at hand" (V.6). This was a time of realization for Paul. He knew it was time for him to depart. He realizes his life is in God's hand and that God's will is being done. One of the most productive responses we can have to our circumstances is to accept them, pain and all. Accepting our pain is an act of faith. It demonstrates that we believe God is in control and is working out His plan for our lives. Paul's departure was also a time of reflection. "I have fought a good fight. I have finished my course; I have kept the faith" (V.7). Paul is reflecting upon his life. He is able to confidently say he has fulfilled his purpose in life. He did what God called him to do. He played by the rules. His reflection indicates he had no regrets. If you realized your departure was at hand, would your reflection be without regrets?

Paul realized his present circumstances reflected upon his past and he looks forward to his future: a time of release. "Henceforth there is laid up for me a crown of righteousness..."(V.8). Paul knew his trouble would soon turn into triumph. His pain would be transformed into power. Paul knew his death was not the end, but rather the beginning of eternal joy. He was about to experience deliverance. He looked forward to his release and his time of reward.

This is a time of realization for all of us. We need to ask ourselves where we are in the context of our ministries, marriages and our Master's plan for our lives. Have we responded to our present pain with faith? What is God asking us to depart from? Have we departed but are still looking back? Or have we forgotten those things which are behind and begun to press forward with purpose, profit, passion and praise? Are we able to reflect with no regrets?

Lessons of life are better learned when caught versus taught. A good model ensures a great masterpiece. Spiritually, everything our Lord asks us to do; He has already done Himself. Not only is He our maker, but He is also our model. More than our foundation, He is our forerunner. Jesus is both our captain and coach. Because Jesus is our model, forerunner, captain and coach, we are to look to Him as we run this race (Heb. 12:2).

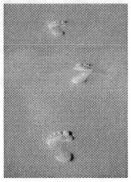

Discouragement is one of the most debilitating attacks of the enemy that we face as we run this Christian race. He purposely sets obstacles before us to sidetrack us. We get concerned with what we see and feel. We begin to analyze and question God's will for our lives. To prevent us from getting side tracked, we must look at our example. Looking unto Jesus, trusting Him continuously for every step. Trusting Him totally instead of relying on self. We must not lean to our own understanding; in all our ways, we are to *acknowledge Him and He shall direct our paths.*

1. **Jesus is our Example**. We are to look to Him in His humanity. He was tempted yet He was without sin. He demonstrated how to run this race with dual natures. He left a legacy for us to follow. He is our Author, the Pioneer of this race. Not only did he start it, He finished it. He perfected our faith. In the midst of the race, we will get discouraged, but Jesus is our example.

2. **Jesus has Experience**. *Who for the joy that was set before Him endured the cross?* (Heb 12:2B) Jesus ran anticipating the prize. He ran with joy because He stayed on course, fulfilling the will of His Father. He ran on God's elected pathway. He endured the cross, despising the shame, knowing that His Father was pleased. Many of us cannot experience joy because we have gotten off of our elected track and out of the will of God. This race is an uphill course, filled with unexpected winds. We must endure, for if we overcome we will be granted the privilege of sitting with Jesus on His throne (Rev 3:21).

3. **Jesus has Given us an Exhortation**. It is inevitable that we get weary in this race. There will be times when our faith will get low. During these times, we are to consider Him that endured contradiction of sinners against himself (Heb 12:3). Consider Him who resisted sin until death (Heb 12:4). Although things may get tough, we have

not resisted unto blood. The exhortation is for us *not to get weary, for in due season, we shall reap if we faint not.*

Look to Jesus as our example, to provide the experience and the exhortation needed to complete this course. Don't give up, give out, or look back. *Therefore, my beloved brethren, be ye steadfast, unmovable, always abounding in the work of the Lord, forasmuch as ye know that your labor is not in vain in the Lord* (I Cor. 15:58).

Man has invented sophisticated weapons of destruction. He has engineered secret, powerful weapons that are invisible to the human eye, yet carry mega power. These weapons are able to destroy a country without notice. In a similar sense, every born-again believer in Christ is frail, fragmented, frustrated on the outside, but has a power source on the inside. This power overcomes our human abilities. Jesus promised He would send Him, the Holy Spirit, who resides within the believer. God lives in us and works  through us. Paul moves us from perspective to power. Perspective is when quitting is not an option. Paul calls the Holy Spirit, who lives in us, the treasure and we are the trash. Our human, frail body, is the vessel that affects our fleshly thinking. There are four powerful components of the secret power within the struggling person.

1. **God Chooses a Fitted Vessel**. Every time we share Christ with an unbeliever, they will get the light of the Word and become a new creation. Everything about us God ordered. We are all unique; our personalities included, we are all different. The body of Christ is composed of different members all joined together by God. He fitted you so that He will get the glory. No one person in Christ has all of the gifts. When you do not work for Christ, your gift is not utilized. Psalm 139:13-16 states that God knew us before we were born; we were fearfully and wonderfully put together. God formed us, called us, sanctified, and changed us.

2. **God Challenges us to be a Faithful Vessel**. 2nd Timothy 2:20-22 tells us, we cannot begin to be faithful until we are first cleaned (self purged). The treasure (Holy Spirit) starts convicting and pushing us towards wanting to be clean. When our lives are dirty, God cannot use us, fully. God wants His vessels to be cleaned. We are all messed up, but God wants a self-motivated heart to push us toward purging our lives, through the power of the Holy Spirit. God also wants us to be prepared for every good work.

3. **God Makes us a Fractured Vessel**. The only way the treasure, the Holy Spirit, can come out, is when God cracks us (hurts us), in order to help us. He wants to deliver us. God will do away with our concept of self. The thing that we hold dear to us, God will take away. The glory will not come out until the garbage is acknowledged. God will crush you to keep you from self and from making wrong decisions. God wants us to totally depend

on Him. We must be fractured before we can be fruitful.

4. **God Channels us to be a Focused Vessel.** When our focus is on the treasure and not on the trash we can be troubled on every side, but we will not get distressed because it is not up to us to get ourselves out of trouble. Every time we say and do things that are not of God, we may get hurt, but those situations will bring us closer to Jesus. There is a power in us that will keep us from giving up. God can change our perspective.

Let's keep our focus on Jesus. "Seek ye first the kingdom of Christ and everything else will be added unto you." When Jesus becomes the center point, everything else will start to fade into the background. Defeats will become victory.

Lessons Which Liberate Us

Life is a series of unexpected changes and challenges. At times, our focus and our faith will dissipate and fall short as our fellowship with God becomes fractured. However, we will soon learn that there is a critical connection between our liberty, learning, leaning, and living. Just when we think we have all things together something else happens. The book of Romans is written by the Apostle Paul on the righteousness of God, through Jesus Christ. This chapter of Romans is trying to teach us that we should put others  ahead of ourselves. This details the edification of the believer. The strong should bear the infirmities of the weak, the education of the Believer (V.4a) which leads to the exhortation that we, through patience and comfort of the Scriptures might have hope. We don't need any more Word. What we need now is to learn how to apply the Word. In the context of II Chronicles 20:17, we need to learn how to fight by faith and when to fight. Some of us are fighting the wrong things.

1. **Learn from our Battles**. Battles will always come your way. We must believe that God is in control, and that Jesus is on the throne. He is working all things together for the good and for those that love the Lord and are His called according to His purpose. We cannot control the storms, trouble is apart of life. Instead of trying to stop our troubles, be still, and know that He is God. The design of the battle is always approved by God. We must also learn the distinction in the battle. What in the battle belongs to you and what part belongs to God? If you are trying to fight God's battle, you will become very weary and frustrated. Our battle is to pray with faith and confidence in God. We must persevere and properly partition God.

2. **Learn from our Bones** (Ezekiel 37). God does not have to change your location to give you an education. Like Israel, we can not see our true condition. With all of your wounds, do you want to be whole? Only the Word will change and transform your life. Your true test is not in the church, but outside. You must come to a place in your life where you recognize that if Jesus does not move on your condition, you are most miserable. Apply the Word to your wounds and you will come out a winner.

3. **Learn from our Brokenness** (Habakkuk 3:17-19). God wants to break us until we submit to His will. The mindset of the Believer is that when God is not doing anything for you, this is a sign of

brokenness. This is when our fight will turn into faith. When we become broken we will not fight, but we will start to agree with the Spirit of God and praise God for who He is. When we are living for Christ, and our minds are on Christ, we will jump over things as He makes our feet like hinds feet. God has to break our wills, wisdom, and words. When we understand the battle, bones, and brokenness, then we will have a breakthrough. He wants us to submit and humble ourselves under the mighty hand of God (I Pet. 5:6). Fully surrender all to Jesus. We need to ask God, "Lord, what will you have me to do?"

Our Observation is an Education

Life tends to liberate people who are willing to learn from their mistakes. One person's problems can become another person's promotion. One person's pitfall can be another person's peace. One's blindness can be another's blessing. In the context of Romans 10, the Jews as a nation are on the bench and out of the game when it comes to salvation. The Gentiles are prospering spiritually because the Jews refused to respond the way God wanted them to respond. As a nation, they will not be saved until we are  raptured out. Then only a small amount of people will be saved. The Church (the Gentiles), listened to what the Jews would not listen to. While they were being sinful and not listening to the testimony of the Prophets, God ushered in the Gentiles.

There are some things that we will listen to and observe. Life allows us to make mistakes, recover, and have a testimony. Hopefully, someone will not make the same mistakes. Although we preach, pray, and plea with people, everyone has to make their own mistakes before they realize what you have said is the truth. You cannot judge people until you have walked in their shoes.

1. **Reasons for Their Rejection** (Rom. 10:1-8). They had problems with Jesus. They were blinded to the truth. They rejected His arrival. In the Church, we are confused. We are so busy trying not too hurt the feelings of others that we have gotten away from the truth. The church is obligated to tell a dark, dying, and hell bound world that Jesus saves. We have a divine command from above, a great commission to go forth with the Gospel, the Good News of Jesus Christ, that He saves. There is also a cry from beneath. There are people in Hell (Luke 16) urging us to get saved and not to come to Hell. We need to come out of the church walls and tell people about Christ. The world rejects Jesus. They rejected that right attitude because they were being so zealous in their own way. They had zeal for God, but not according to knowledge. They had heat, but no light. Heat is emotion, but light is knowledge. Not all emotion represents Jesus. Jesus said we would know them by their fruit. We cannot take for granted that everyone is saved.

2. **Remedy for Their Rejection** (Rom. 10:9). Belief is when God opens up our hearts and minds to know who He is. Jesus is God. He is The Christ, King, and Lord. When we come into His presence, it should be with praise because He has done

more than we can ever imagine. He snatched us out of Hell with smoke still in our garments. God owes us nothing. We cannot say the same thing that God says, believe it in our hearts and our lives show no change. The Word should change the way we walk. There has to be a reception of the message. Faith comes by hearing and hearing by the Word of God. Every time we hear the Word, it should increase our faith. We need the Word.

3. **Results of Their Rejection.** (John 1:11). He came unto His own, and His own received Him not. He made the world, but the world rejected Him. He came unto His own people, the Jews, but they rejected Him. God is rich in mercy. We are not worthy to go to Heaven or to be saved, but He allowed it to happen. This is why we praise His Holy Name. God gave the Jews all the privileges, precepts, power, revelation, and inspiration, but they rejected Christ.

The observation is that by one person's problems, we can have promotion. By one person's pitfall, we can have peace. And by one person's blindness, we can have blessings. Jesus is now saving anyone who puts faith in the finished work of the Lord Jesus Christ. There must be human responsibility in our walk and praise in our obedience. We cannot wait for God to do it all. We must want to do something. We must praise God regardless of what is going on in our lives. Our praise must be genuine. Praise Him because of what He has done. Let everything that has breath, praise the Lord! He is worthy and greatly to be praised!

Nehemiah got permission from the King to go back and rebuild the walls. It took him 52 days to rebuild them. He had a process and a plan. He was met face-to-face by the Samaritans. There are three enemies that will try to stop us from rebuilding our walls. Those three enemies are self, Satan, and our innate sin. These three will stop us, hinder us, and be obstacles to our rebuilding the walls. In every church, righteousness has been destroyed. We have to go back and re-evaluate our walk and our talk constantly.

We have to look at our relationships constantly. We must rely on God and our faith. Nehemiah's plight led to his prayer. Trouble comes in threes: We are either in trouble, just got out of trouble, or are getting ready to go into trouble. Trouble will lead us into prayer.

4. **The Brokenness of the Repentance**. His prayer (V.5). Yahweh means the Covenantal God. We can't even talk to you outside of the covenant you made with Abraham, Isaac, and Jacob. We (Rom. 5), have access according to the blood of Jesus. The only reason we can come boldly to the throne of grace is because of what Jesus did.

Total Recall (An Inspection of Our Reflection)

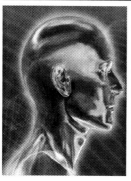

Reflection is a powerful tool of recall. It allows us to access our mindsets and mishaps, trouble and trials, and our wounds and wisdoms of the past. As Paul begins to close the book of Romans, he concentrates on his hindsight's, insights, and foresights of a ministry for Jesus Christ. Paul begins with his gratitude, and ends with God's Glory, but elaborates on his grief. In this context, Paul is not mentioning doctrine, he is talking about personal diligence, which is ministry. Ministry is designed for us to do something for others. At times, we neglect ourselves knowing that at the end, we will receive a reward. Ministry involves influence, to bring people to Christ. It takes an investment of time, talents, and treasures, Ministry includes, inconvenience, involvement, and it is costly.

1. **Paul Expresses his Gratitude** (His Help - vv.1-16). We should never forget those who have helped us get where we are now. In these verses, twenty-seven people helped Paul and sixteen of them were women. One of them was Phoebe, a deaconess who served and ministered as she shielded him from suffering. One couple who helped was Priscilla and Aquila (Acts 18). They risked their lives for his life. In the church, a leader is a servant who models and serves Christ by example.

2. **Paul Expounds on his Grief** (His Hindrances - vv.17-18). Satan comes to divide, divert, and deceive. What can hinder a ministry is not only what Satan does through people from the outside, but also what Satan does through us from the inside. Our personal weaknesses, personal wounds, and lack of wisdom can hinder a ministry. We are all vulnerable and can be used by Satan to go against the Church. How is Satan trying to hinder you from doing God's work?

3. **Paul Exalts his Glory** (His Hope - vv.19-25). Our confidence, our joy, and our comfort is at the end. Weeping may endure for a night, but joy comes in the morning. "Many are the afflictions of the righteous, but the Lord will deliver him out of them all" (Ps. 34:19). Ministry is costly. Through all of the spiritual warfare, all of the labor, and all of the love, look to the end. The end is where Jesus is going to crush Satan under His feet. Satan has already been defeated. You already have the power to stomp him out, in the Name of Jesus. God has not given us the spirit of fear, but of power, of love, and of a sound mind (2 Tim. 1:7).

The problem that most of us have is fear. Fear causes us not to trust in God, even though we are more than conquerors.

Jesus received the victory at the cross, therefore, we are not fighting for the victory; we are fighting from the victory. Satan is under our feet because of what Jesus did at the cross. When Jesus arose on the third day, He got up with all power in His hands There is no power that can stop you. When it comes to our children and other concerns, we need to call things that are not as though they already were. Walk by faith and not by sight. We should stop trembling and start talking to ourselves. We have to know that He is able.

We must know that we have the power of the Holy Spirit. We must know that He that has begun a good work in us will keep on doing it until the day that He returns (Phil. 1:6). We have to know that no weapon formed against us shall prosper. We have to know the Word of God: Jesus is the only man that has all power in His hand. Jesus is Lord! He is Alpha and Omega. Because He lives, we will see God. Jesus the Christ will work out all our problems. Jesus may let Satan work some things in, but ultimately, He is going to work them out. Praise Him for His Person, power and provision.

Watch Where You're Running!

Anyone who has ever tasted victory knows that <u>preparation</u> and <u>perseverance</u> are prerequisites for winning. In the military, it's called basic training. In sports, it's called the minor leagues. In business, it's called development, but in ministry, it's called self-discipline. The writer to the Hebrews has given us *encouragement* throughout the first eleven chapters. Now he concentrates on an event that *expresses* an *exhortation*, but demands the putting away of any *encumbrances* in order to *endure* God's *elected* pathway for our lives.

Each individual initiative presents a different look.

I. **The Event** (<u>Look Out</u>). A mass of people who were faithful in their deportment; people who were tortured fugitivies without fulfillment, win a testimony of being able to say they pleased God. They dramatized on stage for 1,400 years before the world. When Jesus died, the Jewish Program was over. Pentecost in the lower room preceded pentecost in the upper room. God moved to consolidate his redemption program (Jews and Gentiles). Those in the lower room were waiting on righteousness completed. Today, we are saved by righteousness imputed. That's what Paul meant when he said "one Lord, one faith, and one baptism." For an added exhortation, *look out* at the cloud of witnesses.

II. **The Encumbrances and Entanglements** (<u>Look In</u>). The writer alludes to two types of hindrances; weights and sins, which are different from one another.

    A. An Encumbrance (hypnomae) is anything that hinders you from running. This is not, necessarily, something evil, but it keeps us from giving our best to the Lord. Examples: seeking financial security, vacations, nice clothes/cars, fine houses. Seeking success can keep us from putting the Lord first.

    B. Entanglements are sins and works of the flesh, including gossip and gluttony. The sin of unbelief can be is an entanglement because we are running a Race of Faith. This race is not a sprint but a marathon--not a 100 yard dash, but a long distance. It demands perseverance and endurance.

III. **The Elected Pathway** (<u>Look To</u>). In the race that is set before us, God determines the lane we run in and all of the associated suffering. With Suffering He sends a set of Sufficiency and a set Strategy.

Run according to the Exhortation.

Run away from the Encumbrances.

Run with a sense of Endurance.

Run on your Elected Pathway.

Run <u>faithfully</u>, <u>joyfully</u>, and with <u>purity</u> because Jesus ran from Glory to Glory.

Jesus ran in agony from His birth to a barren tomb.

Jesus ran from splendor to sin.

Jesus ran from being our captain to being subjected to cruelty.

Jesus ran from the grave to His Glory.

PRACTICAL LIVING

But be ye doers of the word, and not
hearers only, deceiving your
own selves.

James 1:22

Satan's Deception

And the great dragon was cast out, that old serpent, called the Devil, and Satan, which deceiveth the whole world (Rev 12:9).

Satan's job is to deceive us. When truth is hidden; we are being led by a lie, motives are masked and deception is operating. Satan is always trying to trick, trap us, or tamper with our thinking. Satan got Eve to question the integrity of God, giving her a spirit of dissatisfaction. Motivated by fear, Abraham took matters in his own hands and lay with Hagar. He had a spirit of disillusionment. Moses had a spirit of disobedience when he hit the rock instead of speaking to it as God commanded. We can see throughout the Bible, as well as in our own lives, that Satan has specific strategies to get us out of the will and way of God. He blinds the unbeliever and buffets the believer (II Cor. 4:4). Anyone not rooted and grounded in the Word of God will disconnect when trials and tribulations come. Trouble will either draw us closer to the Lord or drive us away from Him.

Deception is a major tool in Satan's arsenal. Jeremiah 17 describes the heart as wickedly deceitful. It is impossible for us to perform introspection accurately because our heart will mislead us. Only the truth of God's Word can give us an accurate picture of our heart (Heb 4:12). Galatians describes the man who thinks himself to be something when he is nothing, as being deceived. Satan deceives the believer in five major areas: our person, our passions, our principles, our power, and our plans.

Our person is deceived through ignorance of the Scripture. This causes us to intrude into areas God never intended for us to go. My people perish for a lack of knowledge. In II Samuel chapter 6, Uzzah acted beyond his authority when he tried to catch the ark. God killed him. It is dangerous to go into areas for which God has not authorized us. Are you venturing into unauthorized areas? We must guard ourselves so that we do not think we are something when we are nothing, lest we become deceived.

Inappropriateness is the result of being deceived by Satan through our passions. Peter often found himself to be inappropriate because of his passions (Matthew 16, 17). Whenever we become driven by our desires, we will end up in situations that are inappropriate. David's passion for another man's wife caused him to commit adultery and murder. Some of our passions are not legitimate. Instead, they are the result of dysfunction in our lives. Our passions must come under the control of the Holy Spirit in order to avoid being deceived in this area.

The principles of the Word of God are also open to Satan's deception. The result of this deception is iniquity. Peter said, "Ananias, why hath Satan filled thine heart to lie to the Holy Ghost, and to keep back part of the price of the land?" (Acts 5:3). Satan can even use the Word to get us to compromise God's principles. We can be deceived in our perspectives. In I Chronicles chapter 2:1, Satan stood up and provoked David to number Israel. David was deceived in his perspective. It was not God's will to number Israel. We must pray to see things the way God sees them. Our thinking is not always correct. Satan has easy access to us when our thinking is wrong. It is important to have someone in our life that will not be afraid to confront us with truth. We need God's perspective in order to follow His direction and avoid the traps of Satan.

Satan deceives us concerning our power. The result of this deception is insecurity. He tells us we are weak and that we lack the power needed for victory. His job is to keep us from accessing the power that we have on the inside. We have power to call things that are not as though they already were. We have power to overcome bad habits. We have power to access the mercy and grace to help us in our time of need (Heb. 4:16).

Finally, Satan will deceive us in the area of our plans. The steps of a good man are ordered by the Lord. God promises to direct our paths as long as we trust and acknowledge Him. Satan will deceive us by getting us to make decisions without God. What plans have we made without God?

Want to avoid being deceived by Satan? Look for the peace of God, purity of God, principles of God, patience of God and the provisions of God (James 3:17, 18).

The Beauty of Balance

Balance is extremely important for the spiritual maturation of a child of God. Balance allows us to see both sides of the coin. Work must be balanced by rest; talking must be balanced by listening; problems must be balanced by prayer. In Hebrews 12:17, doctrine must be balanced by exhortation. Doctrine is God's truth; it is knowing and believing; however, exhortation is living and obeying. Paul told Timothy to preach and teach. The writer is making a transition while still using the metaphor of running. In order to run successfully, there are 3 major ingredients needed:

1. **A Strong Will** (Needed for *continuance* in this race). Limbs must be strong for the race. "Therefore strengthen the hands that are weak and the knees that are feeble" (Heb. 12:12). The first thing that happens to a runner when he gets tired is, his arms drop. The writer uses this metaphor to describe Israel. The people of Israel had been through a great deal of evil kings, false prophets, rebellious people, etc. So the writer reminds them of the attitude of the kingdom. "When the wilderness and desert will be glad, and they will see the glory of the Lord." Then he reminds them to counsel each other, encourage the exhausted, and strengthen the struggling. Don't give up now; a better day is coming. 1 Peter tells us that our lane (paths) must be straight (1 Pet. 4:12). A track left by the wheels of a cart or chariot creates a path which other travelers follow. When we run, we leave a track behind us, which will lead or mislead others. The lame are the weak, limping Christians who are easily trapped up or mislead. They may be professing Christians who aren't saved, but identify themselves with the Church. Borderline people who are caught between two opinions can become embedded in our lifestyles. We can cause Believers, who are already limp, to be put completely out of joint (spiritual dislocation). Jesus said, "ye are the salt of the earth, but if the salt loses its taste, it's good for nothing." We must maintain a strong *will* of *continuance*.

2. **A Strong Work** (Needed for *diligence* in this race). The writer is speaking about pursuing practical peace and righteousness. Positionally, Believers are already at peace with God, and are dressed in His righteousness. Pursuing peace relates to loving men. In Romans 12:8, Paul says, "if it is possible, live peaceably with all men." Pursuing righteousness relates to loving God. Sanctification is a process that includes purity, obedience, holiness and glorifying God.

3. **A Strong Watch** (Needed for *vigilance in this race)*. We need each other as overseers to encourage us not to give in to temptation, and to prevent a falling out of God's grace, bitterness, and selfishness (Heb. 12:15).

Being Open to Change

When life boils down to the nitty-gritty, the name of the game is *change*. Those who flex with the times, refuse to be rigid, resist the mold, and reject the rut, are the souls distinctively used by God. Change is a challenge; a fresh breeze that flows through the room of routine and blows away the stale air of sameness. As stimulating and invigorating as change can be, it is never easy.

Changes are especially tough when it comes to certain habits that haunt and hurt us. This kind of change is excruciating, but it is not impossible. Jeremiah pointed out the difficulty of breaking into an established life pattern when he said, "Can an Ethiopian change their skin or the leopard its spots? Neither can you do good who are accustomed to doing evil." Notice the last few words, "accustomed to doing evil." In the Hebrew, it means, "Learned in evil". We who are learned in evil cannot do good; evil habits that remain unchanged prohibit us. Evil is a habit that is learned; it is contracted and cultivated by long hours of practice. Jeremiah also says in another place, "I warned you when you felt secure, but you said, I will not listen! This has been your way from your youth; you have not obeyed me." All of us have practiced certain areas of wrong from our youth. It is a pattern of life that becomes "second nature" to us.

We gloss over our resistance, however, with excuses such as, "Well, nobody's perfect," or, "I'll never be any different, that is just the way I am," or, "You can't teach old dogs new tricks." Jeremiah tells us the reason why such excuses come so easily. We have learned to act and react sinfully and unbiblically with ease, and if we admit it, with pleasure. It is essential that we see ourselves as we really are in the light of God's Word, then be open to change where change is needed. The number one enemy of change is the hard-core, self-satisfied sin nature within us. Like a spoiled child, it has been gratified and indulged for years, so it will not give up without a violent temper tantrum. Change is its greatest threat. The flesh dies a slow, bitter, bloody death; kicking and struggling all the way down. Putting off the clothes of the old man (the old, habitual lifestyle), will not be complete until we are determined to put on the garment of the new man. The tailor's name is *change*, and he is a master at fitting your frame.

How to Conquer Sin

If a believer is going to experience the peace, power, presence, and provisions of God, a passion for purity must be developed. We must desire to conquer sin in our lives. That desire comes as we pray for a hatred for sin. I John deals with fellowship and assurance. Our faith is our power, fortitude builds perseverance, and our fight is against perverseness. Although trying to live a clean life is painful, God demands purity. Sanctification is a major part of the believer's life. The Holy Spirit will make changes with or without our cooperation. The believer has three options when it comes to dealing with sin in his life. He can cover it, confess it, and then move toward conquering it through the power of the Holy Spirit.

As we move into the second chapter of I John, knowledge and understanding are addressed. John is writing as a Pastor, providing spiritual direction. We must know and understand that we have a divine capability, a divine comfort, a divine counselor, and we receive divine correction, which leads to divine conduct.

1. **We Have a Divine Capability**. We do not have to sin. Once we accept Jesus into our lives, we have the Holy Spirit on the inside of us. We have also been given a new nature that allows us to respond to His promptings. We are no longer enslaved to sin. We must know Christ and His power, reckon our old nature dead, and yield to the promptings of the Holy Spirit (Rom. 6). This is not automatic. It requires diligence and dedication to have our thinking changed through the Word of God.

2. **We Have a Divine Comfort**. The comfort comes when we mess up. Jesus Christ is our advocate with the Father interceding, speaking, on our behalf. "If any man sin, we have an advocate with the Father, Jesus Christ the righteous" (1 John 2:1b). We can also take comfort that when we don't even know how to pray, the Holy Ghost intercedes on our behalf.

3. **We Have a Divine Counselor**. Jesus satisfies the righteousness, justice, and holiness of God. While what He did was sufficient to cover the sins of the entire world, it is only efficient (it only works) for those whom He has elected. "For whom he did foreknow, he also did predestinate to be conformed to the image of his Son" (Rom. 8:29).

4. **We Have a Divine Correction**. Divine correction operates and allows us to conquer sin, as we are first honest and sincere about our sin. It takes honesty and then obedience. There are three reasons why we obey. We can obey because we have to, because we need to, or because we want to. Maintaining fellowship with God allows our knowledge of Him, and love for Him, to deepen so that obedience is a result of our desire to please Him.

5. **We Have a Divine Conduct**. As we experience divine correction, we will exemplify divine conduct. "But whoso keepeth his word, in him verily is the love of God perfected: hereby know we that are in Him. He that saith he abideth in Him ought also so to walk, even as he walked" (I John 2:5). A direct evidence that we have experienced divine correction, is our ability to love. When our relationship with God is right, then our relationships with others become right.

Do you want to conquer sin? Be honest! Stop covering up. Ask God to give you a hatred for sin and a desire to obey. Start spending time talking to the Lord and reading His Word.

Sex, God's Instrument of Joy

One of the greatest controversies today is one's view of sexual expression. The subject of <u>sex</u> has always been met with widespread opinions, especially within the church. As one examines the <u>Word of God</u>, it becomes apparent that God's views and the world's views are in total contradiction to one another. The world has painted a very <u>twisted</u> and <u>deranged</u> view, whereas God has canvassed and portrayed an awesome and terrific view of sex. Satan depicts an atmosphere of <u>darkness</u>, <u>dim lights</u>, and <u>secrecy</u>, whereas God depicts <u>light</u>, <u>openness</u>, and <u>privacy</u>. As a result of sin and Satan's corrupt concepts regarding God's creation of sex, biblical sexual expression has been twisted and misconceived by the masses. Lies have been developed, indicating that there exists a hush about sex. Birds, bees, and stork stories are mere attempts to avoid God's view. Birds fly, bees sting, and storks do not deliver babies. A child is conceived when sexual intercourse takes place between a man and a woman. Man's sperm engages with an egg released from the woman's ovaries. Life is housed a period of 9 months normally, to produce a person sharing the two personalities of the individuals who originally engaged.

Proverbs 5:15-19 – *"Drink waters out of thine own cistern and running waters out of thine own well. Let thy fountains be dispersed abroad, and rivers of waters in the streets. Let them be only thine own, and not strangers with thee. Let thy fountain be blessed and rejoice with the wife of thy youth. Let her be as the loving hind and pleasant roe; let her breasts satisfy thee at all times; and be thou ravished always with her love."* God's Word provides at least three reasons why God instructed the sexual relationship:

1. <u>Procreation</u>: Genesis 1:28 – "Be fruitful and multiply"

2. <u>Sanctification:</u> I Corinthians 7:9– "It is better to marry than to burn"

3. <u>Satisfaction:</u> Proverbs 5:19 – God uses the word, "know" to express sex.

I would like to suggest that the world's view of sex is twisted, while God's view is terrific.

Satan has twisted at least three areas of sex. He has twisted its:

1. Intent: Lust. Satan's intent is lust – fulfillment (I Cor.10:6; I John 2:16)

2. Interpretation: There is a power behind everything God created. If what God has created is used wrongfully, the power that God instituted will turn on you. (Lev. 18)

3. Initiation: Total depravity. It has psychological and physical judgments. (Rom.1:24; Gen.19)

Unequivocal love: These three expressions find themselves playing out in:

1. Feelings

2. Excitement

3. Jealousy

Twisted (unlawful) sex is terrible for it gets one into trouble with a truthful God. Terrific (lawful) sex is a truthful testing of thanksgiving, and is triumphantly designed to tantalize one's thoughts about God.

At one time we were bound, held down, held back, made to labor; but one day, a Shepherd appeared and made contact with our fore-parents. He expressed His love exclusively, spontaneously, and unequivocally, yet, we still yearn for His appearance. He will return as our King of kings and Lord of lords.

God created sex to be beautiful. Sex was not created to be twisted or full of turmoil. Sex is God's Instrument of Joy.

Stay on the Right Track

Trains run on parallel tracks that give the trains both power and guidance. Without both tracks, the trains could not run. Spiritually, God's righteousness runs parallel to His requirements. If a believer is to find rest and reassurance, both tracks of God's power and man's participation are needed. Too often the Church has been traumatized because we have taught an imbalanced doctrine; we want God to do it all and we do nothing. Everyone that Jesus healed and restored, was required to participate or they would not have been healed. We are discipling and developing people who are spiritually handicapped due to self-inflicted wounds. They want the church to do everything. However, where much is given, much is required.

The parallel tracks apply to our beliefs and our behavior. If we believe the Word of God it has to affect our behavior. Belief and behavior run on parallel tracks. There are three significant situations that have parrallel tracks:

1. **Our Ownership** (1 Cor. 16:1-4). Paul talks about ownership, which we call stewardship. The parallel track of ownership is obedience. The act of giving is an act of our will, as well as, an act of worship. We can give without loving, but we can't love without giving. Upon the first day of the week let every one of you lay by him in store, that's the place (storehouse is the church) as God has prospered him, that's the proportion. The reason ten percent is a starting point and equitable is because it is according to what a person has. In the New Testament there really is no mandate of tithing. Tithing is a starting point because God owns everything, and we own nothing. The word *stewardship* means you are managing the resources of someone else, and there will be a day of reckoning for how you managed these resources. Our ownership runs parallel to our obedience; not only our money, but our time, our treasure, and our talents. As we are obedient, God blesses our ownership. Giving is a part of worship.

2. **Opportunities** (1 Cor. 16:5-10). The parrallel track of opportunities is opposition. Everything in life is predicated on what Jesus Christ allows. Redeem the time, you can't get it back. Time is running out. We must work the works of God while it is day. Every time God allows us opportunity, He also signs off on opposition. When God opens a door, we need to go through

it. We wait for God to open the door we need opened and we should work while we are waiting. The reason God allows opportunity and opposition at the same time is because they keep the "train cars" balanced. It keeps us humble and clean, and makes us conform to the Word.

3. **Obligation** (1 Cor. 16:10-24). Our ability to have open arms to others and to love others is our obligation. Paul moves to some imperatives that are our obligations to openly love one another. Don't let the three things Satan attacks us with 1] Temptations, 2] apathy, and 3] false teachers, preventing us from loving one another with the love that has been shed abroad in our hearts through Christ Jesus.

Your Commission:

Determined by Your Commitment

Military strategists understand the importance of support groups. Support groups are the soldiers in the rear who are not involved in the actual fighting; they support those who are in the direct line of fire. Without proper supplies, support, and sincere reinforcement, devastation would quickly take place. In the spiritual sense, when we begin to look at the Word of God, we need to understand that we must support the work of God so that His kingdom can advance beyond the kingdom of Satan. The Apostle Paul encourages God's people to support the work of God. He recommends a three-fold criterion that will guide us through this process.

1. **God Grants a Sowing Support:** There is a principle for giving. The more we invest in the Lord's work, the more fruit will abound in our lives. As we sow large, we will reap large. When we invest in God's work, our blessings are guaranteed. God does not want an angry giver; He wants a glad giver. Our doctrine will determine our giving. Everyday we sow some kind of seeds; discord, unity, getting or giving... and whatever we put out is what we will get back. "For where your treasure is, there will your heart be also" (Luke 12:34).

2. **God is Glorified by a Serving Support:** We should never make excuses for giving; rather, we should look for opportunities to give. God wants faithfulness. Serving support is needed for the work of the church, in not only what we see, but also in what we do not see. God is glorified in how we give. Giving is not always with our money. What are we doing with our time and talents? When we follow the whole Word of God, He has no choice, but to bless us. Our claim to be a light will liberate us through truth.

3. **God's Gift is for a Sincere Support:** When our prayers are in line with His purpose, they will be answered. When we have a mind-set of giving to support the work of God, the ministry of God, and the Word of God, then God will pour out a blessing in our lives. This is a principle of sowing and reaping. "God will pour out a blessing that you will not be able to receive" (Luke 6:38).

Jesus gave His all on the cross at Calvary. Jesus died for us, and He rose with all power in His hand. God loves a cheerful giver. Whatever we plant will come back. We need people to pray for and with others; to visit, mentor, and help those who have no family. Counsel, sing on the choir, and usher all in the name and to the Glory of Jesus. As you do for Christ, He will do for you. He is faithful.

YOUR WALK

Being confident of this very thing, that He which hath begun a good work in you will perform it until the day of Jesus Christ.

Philippians 1:6

The Liability of Our Logic

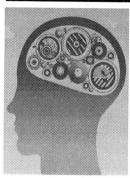

Anyone who totally lives by logic will be lost in his or her attempt to lean on God. His movements are miraculous, mythological, and mysterious. God's designs are strange, but strategic; they are comprehensive, yet complex and progressive, yet powerful. Truly, His ways are not our ways, nor His thoughts our thoughts. He is not a God of human logic. He is the producer of all power. As we look at Jericho, we can see a power, which is more than just a plan and a proposal. We see a God who is working out His will through people who need to depend on Him.

Joshua became great in the eyes of Israel by crossing the Jordan River, but he also was great in the eyes of the Canaanites by taking Jericho. The wall of Jericho did not come down because of walking around it. It came down because they worshipped and bowed down to the Lord. God wants obedience and worship. There are three things which we learn from Joshua's encounter with Jericho.

1. **God has a Mission.** The mission begins with His promise, but there are human responsibilities to be met. We will only be as successful as God gives direction. We need to stop soliciting what He has not intended for us to have. For everything that God wants to do in our lives, we must cooperate. God has the power, but It is your attitude concerning the situation that will determine what happens next.

2. **God has a Method.** God commanded them to march and this march was peculiar. God told them to march quietly, once a day, for six days. This method was probably not logical to some people. Our victory will always involve a test of patience. Count it all joy when you fall into various trials, but let patience have its perfect work. God works in miraculous ways. Do not try to wiggle out of your trials. Many of our prayers will not match up with what God wants to give us. We must learn to pray for God's will, not ours. He is working out our good.

3. **God has Mercy.** The stigma of our sin will follow us, but God looks at our heart and sees our desire to correct the sin in our lives. Rahab, a harlot, is a picture of salvation. She was rescued from destruction. She was justified by her faith. The evidence of her salvation was that she hid the spies. Faith without works is dead. We, the Church, need not be self-righteous. We see other people's sins, but not our own; even if we do not com-

mit the actual sin, what about our hearts? "As a man thinketh in his heart, so is he." There is none righteous, but Jesus.

4. **God has a Mandate**. Take God at His Word. Where there is sin, God will destroy it. He hates sin that affects you and others. Jesus is righteous. We must love the sinner, but hate the sin. God is everywhere and He can see all things. We are in an age where we cannot trust many people. When we are faithful to God, He promotes us.

Learn to be obedient and turn things over to Him. The reason for Joshua's victory was his obedience to God. He worshipped before he went into warfare. We win our battles on our knees.

Cleared by Character

Anyone aspiring to obtain an important position will be thoroughly investigated. Thirty-one years ago, as I entered the Air Force, the specific line of work in which I had been selected required a highly classified clearance. The purpose of this clearance was to ensure the government, that they would not risk a compromise. In a similar sense, when God calls a person into ministry, there are examinations of that person's makeup. Their character, commitment, conviction, and courage become critical conditions for working in God's service. While we begin to walk through the book of Joshua; examining his call, clearance, character, commitment and courage, it is imperative to examine why God selected him to be both Moses' minister and successor. Joshua, the Conqueror of Canaan, can be examined from at least six critical perspectives.

1. **Joshua is Examined as a Son**. (His Home) **Dynamic**-- According to Joshua 1:1, being a son was his first role in life. When Joshua was born, he was named Oshea (Salvation). However, Moses changed his name in Numbers 13:16 to Joshua-Jehoshua. The Hebrew Joshua is the same as the New Testament Jesus. Joshua was the conqueror of evils in Canaan, and Jesus is the conqueror of evils in our lives. Joshua was the firstborn of Non. That meant that on Passover night, Joshua had to be protected by the blood of the lamb.

2. **He's Examined as a Slave**. (His Hindrances) **Destiny**--Joshua was born in Egypt when Israel was suffering under cruel Egyptian rule. Joshua knew all about the injustice of oppresiion against his people. Many times, poverty can help you build moral character. Joshua rose from slavery to be a great conqueror of Canaan. If we expect to conquer our Canaan conflicts, we must have faith that can endure hardship.

3. **He's Examined as a Soldier**. (His Heroism) **Defender**--Joshua is first mentioned as a Soldier. This stemmed from Israel's war with Amalek near Mt. Sinai. Moses appointed Joshua as Israel's military leader to conduct the war against the Amalekites (Ex. 17:9). We learn that as a soldier, he was *proven*. Because he was faithful in small things, Moses gave him greater things.

4. **He's Examined as a Servant**. (His Humility) **Dependent**- -Joshua 1:1 Describes Joshua as a minister of Moses. Deuteronomy 1:38 looks at his character traits. He's <u>humble</u>,

he's <u>honest</u>, he <u>hears</u>, and he's <u>holy</u>. In Ex. 24:13, Joshua was left at the top of the mountain for 40 days. Moses was his hero and role model.

5. **He's Examined as a Spy**. (His Helpfulness) <u>**Duty**</u> -- (Num.13:8) Joshua was chosen to be one of the twelve men to spy out the land of Canaan. This duty required some excellent character traits.

6. **He's Examined as a Successor**. (His Holiness) <u>**Deference**</u>- - Moses prayed for a successor. Prayer helped to reveal the right choice. As Moses kept praying, the Lord answered. (Num. 27:18). Thus, Moses ordained Joshua.

Would you and I receive clearance as a <u>**son**</u>, <u>**slave**</u>, <u>**soldier**</u>, <u>**servant**</u>, <u>**spy**</u> and <u>**supplicator**</u>?

Displaced Light

Light throughout the Bible has always been a preview of the person, presence, power, and purposes of God. God's light transcends life; it exposes us to truth, transformation, and tranquility; and it renders us humbled when we enter His presence. Those in the Bible who approached God were mystified at this light. God is light. As we study the parables, we find ourselves dealing with this dynamic mention of God's light.

The definition of a parable is a comparison or contrast of two things. It illustrates truth by analogy. When Jesus spoke in parables, His whole intent was for people not to understand. It was for the disciples to understand, for they were secrets to the kingdom and the kingship of Jesus Christ. In Matthew chapter 5, Jesus is teaching the Sermon on the Mount. He is giving clarity on truths for the kingdom. In Matthew 5:1-16, Jesus lays out the true righteousness that is connected with the kingdom of God, which Jesus will set up at His earthly reign. He is forecasting the principles that will be mandated on earth at the time of Christ's earthly kingdom. Jesus gives four attitudes:

1. **An Attitude of Ourselves** (vv.1-3). Jesus says, Blessed are the poor in spirit (those who are humble). In other words, happy is the person who is not self-inflated.

2. **An Attitude toward Sin** (vv.4-6). Blessed are they that mourn (over their sins). We should be preoccupied with mourning over our own sin and seeing it as God sees it. When we keep looking at the sin of others, we don't see our own.

3. **An Attitude toward the Lord** (vv.7-9). Blessed are the merciful and the peacemakers. We receive God's mercy and peace as we trust Christ and He wants us to show mercy and peace toward others.

4. **An Attitude to the World** (vv.10-16). Blessed are they who are persecuted. The world will always be in conflict with the Christian. We need not feel bad when the world does not accept us. If we are living right, they ought to reject us. If we blend right in, something is wrong with our testimony.

There are four powerful premises that come out of this study on "light."

(1) *There is a purpose for our light*. This light is an enrichment to the world. We are light bearers because we have God's light in us. Satan rules this world system. We are lights in a darkened world.

(2) *There is a placement of God's light.* Jesus says, "A city set on a hill cannot be hidden" (V.14). In other words, we have been set in a particular place to be witnesses. What hinders our witness to the world? First is disruption from fellowship, second is doctrinal error. Faith that does not preach Jesus as God, is in error.

(3) *There is a power of God's light*. Jesus says, "Neither do men light a candle and put it under a bushel but on a lamp stand and it gives light to all that are in the house" (V.15). This is speaking of the empowerment of light. God has given us the ministry of reconciliation. This is where we are able to bring liberty to the captives and power to the prisoners. When God's light is properly placed, it gives light to the whole house (our dwelling place). Thus, we are watchmen for our own house.

(4) *There is a visibility to God's light*. Jesus says, "Let your light so shine that others may see your good works, and glorify your Father who is in Heaven" (V.16). Let our enlightenment be a teaching tool for others who are watching us. Our transformed life should speak for us. This transformed life (our walk, talk, dress, etc.), comes from being in God's presence. We must learn to let our lights of enlightenment and transformation shine. This will cause others to "glorify your Father who is in Heaven." We must be a witness to the world, a watchman for our homes, and a worshipper of God before all men. To accomplish this, we must make sure that our light is not displaced, but in the right place. The light is Jesus Christ. We are light bearers of Jesus Christ!

Led or Lied To

The guidance of the Holy Spirit is one of the most confusing ordeals for the people of God. Being lead of the Spirit is a form for one's feelings, and a fascination for one's fictions. As we design a philosophy of being in God's place of guidance, we must understand the significant initiatives that are in place when God is guiding us.

Who is the Holy Spirit and what is His function? He is a person who possesses an intellect. He has a will and has feelings. He can also be grieved. He is the third person of the Godhead. His chief function is to glorify Jesus Christ. He converts, convicts, convinces, and constrains the believer. He restrains evil, indwells, fills, heals, baptizes, prays, and strengthens us. In the Old Testament, He was a Cloud that led Israel by day and a Pillar of Fire by night. Paul, in Romans 8:14 says, "For as many as were led by the Spirit of God they are the sons and daughters of God." Some claim to be led by God, but what they claim God used to lead them was against Scripture. Whenever God leads, it will never conflict with Scripture. If God is not leading you, you are being detoured.

1. **Conformity to His Principles**: The Word of God must be our wisdom for victory. Sometimes God will not move you from your situation, but will give you certain assurances that in the midst, He is still operating. God will give you truth. When things happen in our lives, we need to ask, "Lord, what are You trying to say to me about myself and what do You want me to do?" Everything has a purpose. God expects us to live a life of trust. There must be a platform that is in line with His principles.

2. **Calm of an Inner Patience**: He will give us patience to abide under His providence, as we grow through trials. God will guide as He prospers. Prosperity is when God opens doors for us. He allows us to benefit from our bad conditions. When He is leading us, there is no fear. Even through warfare, we are waiting for our deliverance because of the eternal power indwelling us. God is preparing in us a fire to consume what is before us. God was preparing Moses, who was frustrated, had no confidence, was not self-reliant, but still, he was where God wanted him.

3. **Consolation of God's Peace**: Peace works with patience, which builds up faith and character. Peace on the inside keeps us from agitation because of what is happening on the outside.

The peace of God that surpasses all understanding will keep your hearts and mind through Christ Jesus (Philippians 4:7). God put a guard on our hearts and minds. The mind protects our thoughts and the guard protects our feelings and emotions. Peace holds everything together.

4. **Certainty of His Promises**: When you are in a bad situation, you do not need to see to believe, but must know that all things work together for the good of them who love God and are called according to His purposes. The promises are designed to promote us. We cannot see where God is going to use us, until we are in trouble and then God will show us His promises through His Word.

5. **Comfort of His Presence**: God's presence is our protection. "Yea, though I walk through the valley of the shadow of death, I will fear no evil" (Ps. 23:4). In the valley is depression, discouragement, darkness, and unseen enemies, but we are protected and promoted through His presence.

Are we led or lied to? Are we in the place of guidance, walking according to His will, living according to His Word, and doing things according to His way? He is worthy to be praised. Are we in the place of God?

Life is Subject to Change

Anyone who has walked with the Lord, knows God has engineered our pathways according to His will. We are not given previews of the pathways God chooses for us. Faith is operating in our lives, not because we know what tomorrow holds, but because we know who holds tomorrow. We will undoubtedly experience times of joy and prosperity, as well as times of distress and trouble. God is sovereign and does not owe us an explanation. We may often wonder why this, why me, why now? Simply put, He is working out His will in our lives. Scripture teaches us to "give thanks in everything for this is the will of God in Christ Jesus concerning you" (I Thes. 5:18).

We have no guarantees. Life can change in a moment. Consequently, we must number our days and redeem the time. In the thirteenth chapter of Joshua, God, without notice, brings about major changes in Joshua's life. In the first twelve chapters, Joshua is a conqueror and military general. In the last twelve chapters, he is a commissioner and a governor. His whole direction is changed. Typically, we do not respond well to change. God wants our focus and faith to remain constant in the midst of changing circumstances.

The last half of the Book of Joshua opens with his assignment. "Now Joshua was old and stricken in years" (13:1). God is dealing with Joshua's aging, reminding him he still has work to do. This was Joshua's door of opportunity. God does an assessment of Canaan: there still remains, much land to be possessed. Now is the time to serve. It is not the will of God to sit, but to serve. There still remains kingdom work to be done. Are you sitting or serving? Don't wait until your door of opportunity closes.

God first gives assurance to Israel and then the assignment (V. 6). "All the inhabitants of the hill country . . . I will drive them out." He gives them promise, perspective, and placement. When God assigns us to a work, He always gives us assurance. "He who hath begun a good work in you shall perform it until the day of Jesus Christ."

Joshua is now required to be administrator. He is given a mandate, a method, and a moment to divide the land (vv.6-7). The method of dividing is by lot. The mandate was God's command. The moment was now. The administration of Joshua begins with a declaration of his leadership, which leads to the dividing of the land (vv.8-33). Joshua divides the lots according to God's design. Whatever God gives us is by His design. Our blessings, just like Caleb's inheritance (Jos. 14:9-13), are based upon the Word, our walk, and our witness.

Finally, he has to deal with the delinquency of the people. The first area Joshua confronted was weakness (Jos. 15:63). Weakness, or a propensity toward things that are reprehensible to God, can block our blessings. Compromise is the second area that can prevent us from receiving blessings (Jos. 17:13). The third area was procrastination. We need to consider, is weakness, compromise, or procrastination blocking our blessings?

We are reminded that the Book of Joshua deals with the walk of the believer. The second half of Joshua's life provides us a lesson on how to handle change. We need to stop trying to get rid of everything in our lives. We must learn to stand still and see the salvation of God. Life is subject to change without notice. If it changes, don't get aggravated; instead, receive His assurance and accept His assignment.

A Mandate for Ministry

One of the greatest transformations a child of God will go through is the changing of the mind. It is nothing short of a miracle of how God impacts our thinking when we come to the saving knowledge of Jesus Christ. When we are truly born again, the things we used to do, we no longer desire to do. God affects our desire and redirects us.

We are not saved until we repent. With repentance comes a change of direction. Salvation is of the Lord, through pre-destination and by the selection of the Holy Spirit (Eph.1). Salvation impacts us only when God chooses and calls us. We respond through repentance and recognizing that we need a Savior. Once saved, the Holy Spirit takes residence on the inside and then He changes us in stages.

When there is no desire to change, we can Biblically question our salvation. A changed life is evidence of salvation. Being saved does not mean perfection, or that we will not make mistakes or return to our old ways. What it means is that we cannot continue to practice sin. There should be an overwhelming desire and conviction to do what is right. In this context, Paul is challenging us to embrace and accept each other. Ministries in the church should be a model of Christ, which is to serve and not sit.

1. **We Must Meet the Requirements**: What we believe should have ramifications on our lifestyles. Our lives should be challenged daily to transform our minds and to walk in the light as Christ is in the light. We will make mistakes, but the more we walk with God, the more we will understand His motives in the Scriptures. This will help us to change our thinking. What comes out of our mouths and what goes through our minds, should be for the Glory of God. We tamper with God's Glory when we say things and think things that are contrary to Scripture. In spite of our disagreements, we need to pursue spiritual harmony.

2. **We Must Manifest a Reception**: If the sinless Son of God could receive us as sinners into His family, why can't we lovingly embrace one another and receive others into our family? There is no room for "cliques" in the Body of Christ. We must stop separating ourselves in the Church and tell people about Jesus. The Church is silent concerning same-sex marriage and other sin issues. The Church's silence indicts the Church. Somebody should be preaching a prevalent, powerful Christ-

centered message and stop preaching about prosperity, supernatural healing, and ruining the Holy Spirit, while the unsaved are going to hell. Jesus is going to hold us accountable because we are the light and salt of the world. Start talking about Jesus.

3. **We Must Move the Barriers of the Redeemed**: If we say we have the truth in our minds then our behaviors should be affected. There is a connection between the mind and behavior, truth and virtue. The Church needs to stop playing games. Either we are in or out. Judgment will begin in the House of God. The barriers in the Church must come down.

4. **We Must be Motivated to be Refreshed**: When we are saved, we are under the inspiration and influence of the Holy Spirit. In Him there is one faith, one power, one baptism and one God. Jesus sends the Spirit of God into the people of God and fulfills HIs position as High Priest, by interceding for us.

We are edified and we have joy. We are refreshed and we can go through trials and not give up. It is the flow of the Holy Spirit that keeps us going. His mercy is new every morning. He is faithful. He is a God that has all power in His hand.

Every knee shall bow and every tongue shall confess that Jesus is Lord to the Glory of God. We must forget about ourselves. Let the church have the same mind, same mouth and the same ministry in Christ. Let's unify; let's love one another even in the midst of our differences. Dwell on things that are positive. Let us love one another in Christ.

Placed by His Providence

One of the unique privileges of the people of God is that we are providentially placed by God as it pleases Him. God determines our place, position, and parameters to serve in this life. He determines our gifts, placement, and pace in the race. This placement gives us a sense of peace and power as we perform His will. God places us where He wants us. Where God has placed us, we did not pray to be there. (It is then that we think we have to make things happen to stay in the place where He has us).

In the context of Daniel, we will see the divine placement, the faithfulness, fortitude, and future blessing of the Nation of Israel. We will see that God is the God that rules. The first seven chapters cover Daniel's personal history. The prophesy of Daniel is found in Chapters 8-12. Daniel had an inner conviction to stay with God through adverse situations. The book of Daniel also depicts Gentile world rule. We are all providentially placed by God in our churches. God places us here to do ministry and to exalt His Name. There is a five fold initiative of being placed by God.

1. **Placed by God for a Purpose** (Dan. 1:1-8).The King wanted children who would enhance his kingdom; Daniel was chosen. God gave him the power to prevail. Daniel would not compromise his commitment to God's will. The church needs people of purpose who will reach, teach, and disciple. God will test us with little, to see if our faithfulness is right, before He gives much. We must purpose in our hearts that the Word of God stays pure. We must give Christ order and excellence.

2. **Placed by God for a Principle** (Dan. 1:9-21). We are no longer under Grace by ceremonial laws. These verses are not so much about food, but they are about faith and how God gifted Daniel with dreams and visions. Whatever power we have comes from God. God determines all positions, because He rules. We can rest, knowing that He is in control. Be still and know that He is God.

3. **Placed by God for Prescription** (Dan. 2). Daniel used his gifts to glorify the God of Heaven. He trusted God. When we trust God, He will work out our good for His glory. God will not always take us out of undesireable situations. He is able to bless us, and give us rest, reassurance, and reward in the midst of the situation.

4. **Placed by God for a Pitfall** (Dan. 3). Daniel had three friends, Shadrach, Meshach and Abednego. God was sending a message, "You can put my people in a furnace, but they will never burn." Because of their dedication to the Lord, they were willing to die rather than to sacrifice their conviction. Our test of dedication is a refusal to compromise what we believe, even when pressure is on us. Our faith will cost us something in our homes, jobs, marriages, and in our minds, but stand for Jesus and don't move. God is able to bring you out without a scratch. Yes, even if we die, He will deliver us. When Jesus is on our side, we can be placed in any furnace and He will bring us out. He will be our protection, our provision, our peace, and our God in the midst of trouble.

5. **Placed by God for Praise** (Dan. 4). When we know that it is God that set up everything in our lives; even in the midst of the fiery furnace, we just need to know that He is able to keep us. We are not here because we are good, it is all about Jesus and Him crucified. We must stay where God has placed us.

It is not the furnace, but the faith that gives us a sure foundation, which is Jesus Christ. He is able to keep us from falling and to present us faultless. Ministry is not a job, it is a calling. We must be faithful where God has called us.

A Proposition of Poison

Everyday there are propositions between individuals, organizations, and companies. These propositions are proposals to enact a business deal between two entities. Lawyers take months to weed through the fine print. In a similar sense, Satan is so strategic that he has initiatives that look innocent; but when we read the fine print; there is some language out of hell that has been intertwined in the agreement. According to Gen. 1:1, God created something perfect, but by verse 2, the earth was without form and void. Satan brought about chaos and confusion, but the Spirit of God moved across the face of the deep and brought order. The Spirit of God also calls order out of disorder in our lives. To do this, the Spirit has a threefold initiative:

1. **The Holy Spirit wants to move the child of God from an independence from God.** He does not want the child of God to become independent in his thinking. Satan wants us to buy into his proposal that we can do things without God. In Matthew 3, as Jesus is baptized, God gives His approval—This is my beloved Son, in whom I am well-pleased (Mt. 3:17). When we are approved by God, we have an appointment; we are approached by Satan to be tempted. God takes us through something, and proves Himself in us by giving us power in the midst of the problem. Matthew chapter 4 tells us that Jesus was led up by the Spirit. Jesus had an appointment in the place of His testing. Jesus, after fasting 40 days, was hungry. Satan wanted Jesus to act independent of the Father, but Jesus did not cheat by turning stones into bread.

2. **The Holy Spirit wants to move us from Satan's dangerous impact.** Satan moves in three major areas of our lives. First, he gives us no freedom from our fear. Fear is *"False Evidence that Appears Real."* We have a fear of the unknown, of the future, of rejection, etc. However, God has not given us a spirit of fear but of power, of love, and of a disciplined mind. Psalm 23, the Shepherd psalm, is the antithesis of fear; it is about faith in the Shepherd. With the Shepherd, we have no fear; no fear of a lack of rest, no fear of thirst, no fear of a lack of joy, no fear of the future, no fear of loneliness, no fear of the lack of comfort, no fear of hunger, no fear of predators, and no fear of our past catching up with us. When fear comes into the camp, faith has said good-bye. Second, Satan gives us no freedom from our fractures. 2 Cor. 10 tells us that we need God's weaponry

to deal with our inward fractures. We must allow the Spirit of God to deal with them. Satan uses our fractures to keep us from the will of God, but God tells us to cast down imaginations and everything that would exalt itself against the knowledge of God (2 Cor. 10:5). Third, Satan gives us no freedom from false hopes. Jer. 2:13 tells us that Israel left God (the fountain of living waters) and did their own thing (cisterns that were broken and could hold no water). Our stuff is full of holes!

3. **The Holy Spirit wants to move us from our impulses.** Satan wants us to make a decision based on our impulses rather than wise counsel. Then, we develop a plan outside the will of God's purpose. On the other hand, the Holy Spirit moves us from impulses to wisdom as we make our decisions.

Quitting is Not an Option

Quitting is never an option for the Believer. It is an out for those who feel like outcasts. People who desire to quit are typically living on the edge of psychological desperation. Quitters become tired of the tumultuous terrain of trouble. We all need to develop a theology for trouble. Life is not a bed of ease. We can't keep naming it and claiming it. There are some valleys and mountains, but the fuel of faith is trouble. What keeps us going is that God is able to transform us through the troubles from the outside. In spite of our pain, disturbance of plans, and even poverty-stricken provisions, the Apostle Paul gives us, as Believers, three powerful platforms as to why we should persevere. When we come face to face with a quitter, their love is limp, their consciences are crippled and their faith is fractured. Becoming tired is only human, and we get tired when we try to do things in and of our own strength. Paul points out three motivations in us through Christ, that will not let us quit.

1. **We Must Be True to our Appointments (Ministry).** Why do we continue to go on and not faint? We may feel like quitting, but if we know Jesus, we will not quit. God has entrusted to us a ministry of service in His Name. We must keep ministering to others. Others are depending on us and we cannot quit. God can't work through us until He pulls something out of us. We have a glory that He wants us to share. Let your light so shine. The gospel of Jesus Christ leads to growth and He helps us to help others to grow. We have a ministry in Jesus Christ.

2. **We Must be Thankful for our Appropriations (Mercy).** We can't quit because we are obligated to Jesus. He has much mercy for us. Some people feel that God did not show them much mercy. Many of us have said and done things that should not have been said or done. Because of our mindsets and mouths, we have driven others away. We hurt those closest to us because we do not like ourselves. We must stop holding others hostage because of our historical issues. God had mercy on us and forms a pattern in us to get us to win others to Himself. Mercy keeps us going, builds up our transparency, keeps us humble, keeps us out of pity parties, and away from self-centeredness. When we understand that Jesus has forgiven us for everything, then we will feel obligated to reach others for Jesus Christ.

3. **We must be Tolerant of our Approvals (Motivations)**. God allows warfare. In the Old Testament, God was trying to teach Israel trust and dependence, so God allowed the enemy to come after His own people. He wanted His people to stand still and call out to Him (2 Chronicles 20). Before the battle begins, it has already ended.

God wants us to trust Him. He is too wise to make a mistake. We need Jesus to give us the strength, faith, fight, fruit and victory because He is our Deliverance and Healer. The weapons of our warfare are not carnal, but mighty through God to the pulling down of strongholds. Strongholds are things that keep us in bondage. When the strongholds are loosened, we are free to think right, talk right, and walk right. We can't quit because we have power through Christ Jesus. *Stop quitting and be quiet.*

Spiritual Closure

Closure is one of life's certainties. Every beginning has an ending and every start has a finish. Sunrises close with sunsets. Each prologue concludes with an epilogue. Spiritually, our lives have closure. Our spiritual closure should bring glory to God. It is not about what we were, but what we shall be. How will we be remembered? Will we be remembered as one who helped or one who hindered? Did we serve or want to be served? Our lives, did it exalt Christ or attempt to exploit Him? How will we go out?

Paul brings closure to this in a letter to the Galatians, in the sixth chapter. He finalizes his instructions with a signature, a summary and a storyline. His conclusion deals with graphics, grace, grief, and God's glory. The signature of Paul authenticates the letter to the Galatians. "You see how large a letter I have written unto you with mine own hand" (V.11). Paul is making a statement of the personal effort made to complete this letter because of the importance of the instructions contained within it. Through this graphic description of his signature, Paul is saying, "don't miss this letter." He takes a final opportunity to elevate grace over works (V.12).

The summary of the letter expresses Paul's grief (vv.12-13). He argues against and warns the Galatians about the Judaizers. For the ones who are circumcised do not keep the law; but "they desire to have you circumcised, that they may glory in your flesh" (V.13). The instruction and influence of these Judaizers grieved Paul because they were men pleasers and boasters. They desired to win converts to fuel their boasting. Paul called them compromisers, persuaders, and even hypocrites. Galatians ends with Paul's story line. The story line that Paul wants us to understand is that it is not about us. It is about the Glory of God. "But God forbid that I should glory, save in the cross of Lord Jesus Christ, by whom the world is crucified unto me, and I unto the world" (V.14). Paul understood and knew the person, power, purpose, and persecution associated with the cross. Paul's knowledge of Christ, the person of the cross, was not casual but personally intimate; consequently, he was fully acquainted with the power of the cross to give new life. "That I may know him in the power of his resurrection and the fellowship of his suffering."   The purpose of the cross was to eliminate national, cultural, and racial distinctions: "for in Christ neither circumcision availeth anything nor un-circumcision, but a new creature" (V.15).

Finally, Paul understood the persecution of the cross. "We are troubled yet not distressed...perplexed, yet not in despair...persecuted but not forsaken, cast down but not destroyed." The persecution associated with the cross is God's way of branding us. If we want to reign with Him, we must suffer with Him. Don't miss the story line. It's all about God's Glory. Do we know the person of the cross? Are we experiencing the power of the cross? Do we understand the purpose of the cross? Are we willing to go through the persecution associated with the cross? How will we go out? Live everyday and do everything to the Glory of God!

When It's Right, It's Rough

During the late 1960's there was an intriguing television program filled with espionage, clever disguises, penetration into enemy territories, and innovative strategies. The program, Mission Impossible, always opened with two statements; an option and a promise. The option was, "your mission, should you choose to accept" and the promise; "this tape will self-destruct." God has a mission and plan for each of us. Our mission, should we choose to accept it, includes attacks, frustration, and inconvenience. The promise is, "Satan will inevitably self-destruct." If we accept the calling and carry out the will and vision God has for our lives, we will be victorious. Chapters two through five of the Book of Joshua contain a biblical strategy for victory. The Promised Land represents victory for the Believer.

1. **It is a Mission of Caution.** Spies were sent on a secret mission to view the land. When God sends us on a mission, He has already performed what is needed; however, there is still personal responsibility. We must be cautious, understanding what is going on around us. We cannot remain ignorant of the enemy's devices or our own personal weaknesses. Our mission requires watching and prayer. We need not only watch what is going on around us, we also need to watch what is happening within us. Whenever we are over confident, we are outside of the will of God.

2. **It is a Mission of Conflict.** Men pursued the spies (Josh. 2:7,8). Acceptance of God's mission for our lives will always lead to conflict. We can expect to have our family and finances come under attack. Our response should be to count it all joy. Our trials lead to testimonies, and our trouble is translated into triumph as we are transformed by it. God's mission will always lead to warfare. Even in the midst of warfare, we are to give thanks knowing that God has a plan, a purpose, and program for our lives.

3. **It is a Mission of Courage.** Rahab saw what God had done for His people and was willing to risk her faith and family on Him. Faith is courageous. Rahab's courage led to confession and worship. Because of the great works God had done for His people, she knew she could not place any confidence in herself. Instead, her confidence and courage was in the God

of Israel. We can be of good courage when we know the outcome is dependent upon the Most High God.

4. **It is a Mission of Choice**. Rahab chose to help the spies. Faith allows us to receive the wisdom of God, so that we can make the right choice. Her choice brought about protection and provision for her and her family. Although we will be faced with some tough choices during our mission, if we learn not to lean on our own understanding and acknowledge the Lord, He will direct our paths.

5. **It is a Mission of Confidence**. Truly the Lord has delivered into our hands all the land; for even all the inhabitants of the country do faint because of us (2:23). Our confidence is not in us, but in the Lord.

6. **It is a Mission of Consecration** (3:7,8). God can do great things through us and in spite of us, if we are willing to live holy and consecrated lives. Joshua's consecration led to his exaltation. Are you willing to be set apart for the glory of God?

7. **It is a Mission of Commitment**. We must be committed to God's process. Failure to go through His process is disobedience. Our commitment is demonstrated as we persevere. Even in the rough places God is still in control and has a perfect and divine plan for our lives.

We must accept our mission and be victorious. However, we should proceed with caution; watching as well as praying, be prepared for the conflict, demonstrate courage, exercise faith so that we can make right choices, place confidence in the God of our salvation, live a holy and consecrated life before God so that He may get the glory, remain committed to the process and experience victory!

SANCTIFICATION

And such were some of you: but ye are
washed, but ye are sanctified, but ye are
justified in the name of the Lord Jesus, and
by the Spirit of our God.

1 Corinthians 6:11

It is Time to Wake Up

Whenever God wants to re-direct our paths, capture our attention, or discontinue our involvement in a certain area of life, He sends a wake up call. Wake-up calls are designed to enlighten the believer about their commitments. They come because we have missed God's message of direction. Wake-up calls keep us from drifting, doubting, and becoming dull to the Word of God. They help us get back on the path that God has originally directed for our lives. God is concerned when the seed of the Word has not  hit the soil of our hearts. God wants to shake us and wake us up to His Word and to His way. Many of us do not want to hear from God unless we are in dire need of Him.

In the context of 2 Corinthians, Paul wants to have a heart to heart talk with the church at Corinth. They have become blind in their walk, work, warning, and their willingness to serve.

1. **A Wake-up Call for their Service** (2 Cor. 6:1-10): Paul feels that the Corinthians do not really appreciate him. They would rather listen to unbiblical doctrine. Paul wants them to know that salvation is needed today, not tomorrow, and that it is only Jesus that saves. Not everyone in church is saved. Things that are being done in the Church today are not all apart of God's plan. We cannot compromise the Word. There is only one Lord, one faith, and one baptism. We cannot let our disobedient walk affect others. We must not become a stumbling block to others. We are being watched by unbelievers. How are we supporting the efforts of God? We have an obligation to do a work for the Lord and to develop the Body of Christ.

2. **A Wake-up Call for their Separation** (2 Cor. 6:11-17): We should not be unevenly yoked with unbelievers in business or relationships. Separation is not just isolation from someone because of what they do; it's about our sanctification through Jesus Christ. It is about our motives and our desires. The nature of the unclean is different from the clean. When we link up with unsaved people, we are really not attracted to the same things. The natures are different. We all make mistakes, but we are warned not to become unevenly yoked, and mingle with the unsaved. How can two walk together unless they both agree? It is difficult. When relationships fall apart, the only way to repair it is with honesty, the Bible, and with love.

3. **A Wake-up Call for their Surrender** (2 Cor. 7): There must be a surrender to God's wisdom. We must deal with our problems honestly. It takes two to make a difference. God wants us to reconcile with each other. It is not God's will for you to come to church and have situations in your life that you have not reconciled. Reconciliation will cost you humility, truth, love, and the loosening (forgiveness) of that individual. Let us not go another day with wrath in our lives. Surrender to the Word and to the Will of God.

Court is in Session

Most parents become very angry when their children are willful, rebellious, and obstinate in their behavior; when their children reject their love and are openly disobedient. Oftentimes when children display that kind of attitude, there are consequences that are very unpleasant. In a similar sense man, from the very beginning, has had an openly rebellious, obstinate rejection of God's love. As a result, we have seen God's righteous indignation.

We do not want to hear about what is really bothering God. If we can attend church every Sunday, go home and watch X-rated movies, rent videos where there is much cursing, and are not bothered by it, can we call ourselves Christians? Something should bother us. If the Spirit of God is living inside of us, there is no way that we can be tolerant of unadulterated mess. Jesus said, "You will know them by their fruit", not by their Sunday suits.

There are four parts to God's Day in court:

1. **The Reason for God's Mood is His Anger**. God shows His anger by letting the law of the harvest take place. Mankind is intelligent. He decides to ignore God, and then he indulges in what he wants without repentance. Therefore, the true Church of Jesus Christ needs to evangelize a dark, dying, and hell bound world.

2. **The Refusal of God's Manifestation is His Attributes**. Man is a deliberate rebel. It is a willful decision to become a homosexual. Idolatry proceeds immorality. When we practice immorality, we make something or someone our god. When God does not give us everything that we want, it is in our best interest. When we are in the right place, believe in the right Person, and live out the principles of God, we and our families are blessed.

3. **The Reality of God's Deliberate Mishaps**. When we reject Jesus, the Word of God, God's Way and the true Church of Jesus; then He will start to abandon us. The result is that we are not free. We are only free when God has us. When God lets us go, we become a slave to our own lusts. Our lusts become a boomerang.

4. **The Doom and the Devolution.** Once our minds becomes

reprobate, we can never get back. We are locked into Hell. When we are of a reprobate mind, we are filled with all manner of unrighteousness.

The reprobate are not ashamed; they have pleasure in what they are doing. God is going to have the last say so. Be not deceived, God is not mocked. God knows that we are not perfect, but when we are washed we do not want to go the way of sin any more. He gives us a different mind set, and a different desire. We want to try to please the Most Holy God, and walk in the Light as He is in the light. Well, the court is in session and here comes the judge. Jesus is Judge, the Jury and the Lawyer. When He represents us, He will throw our cases out of court. But we have to be saved, then sanctified, and satisfied.

Death is a Door to Deliverance:

I Am Crucified with Christ

Technology is a blessing from God, which allows us to live in a less stressful environment. As a result of technology, we are privileged to walk through automatic doors, use automatic icemakers, and click remote controls for our TVs. We are also blessed with answering machines and cell phones. However, with all this technology and automation, we seem to have lost our work ethic.

Spiritually, our sanctification is not automatic. In our position in Jesus Christ, when we were saved, we were sanctified and seated automatically in heavenly places. However, in our practice on earth, we have to work out our salvation. God works in us, and now the Holy Spirit wants to work what is in us, out of us. If we are going to live right, be right, think right, and walk right, it will take our participation. Although we are not working for salvation, we are working from salvation.

One of the dynamics of experiencing the power, peace, provisions, and protection of our minds, is for us to be crucified with Christ. Though Christ is already Lord, He wants us to let Him rule in our lives. We can never have the joy, the power, the peace, or the sense of belonging until we come under God's jurisdiction and become crucified. Part of being free is to go through the process of crucifixion because we are predestinated to be conformed to the image of Jesus Christ.

The thrust of Galatians is our justification by faith and the sanctification, which accompanies it. Part of the freedom that this brings is to be crucified. That is, putting aside one's desires and sacrificially living for the Lordship of Christ. Jesus said, "to come after Him one must deny himself, take up his cross, and follow Him" (Luke 9:23). Thus, Galatians 2:20 begins with the denunciation of self: "I am crucified with Christ."

There are four criteria for Crucifixion:

1. **Definition for Crucifixion.** Crucifixion means a rejection of the world's system and how it operates. In other words, my agenda is no longer to be rich, famous, or powerful, it is now to glorify the Name of Jesus. Hence, the definition for crucifixion is self-denial.

125

2. **Design for Crucifixion**. In Rom. 6, Paul says that there is an indwelling union between Christ and us. In a once and for all act in the past, we died with Christ and rose with Christ. Therefore, we are told that we are dead to sin (V.1). There are four aspects to our death to sin; First, there is an operation of God in which those of us who are in Christ have died with Christ to the power of sin. We can say "no" to sin. Second, there is an education (vv.6-10). Paul wants us to know that our old man is crucified with Christ so that we do not have to serve sin. Third, in verses 11-13 we have the application. We must present ourselves as a living sacrifice because God has given us the ability to come out of the world. Fourth, is the elimination (V.14) process. This means that sin does not have dominion over us. Through crucifixion, God has given us a design and a desire to want to live for Him.

3. **Difficulty of Crucifixion**. According to Col. 3, since we are raised with Christ, we are to seek the things that are above (V. 1). We are to set our affection on things above, not on the things of the earth (V.2). Then we are to subtract fornication, idolatry, anger, etc (V.5). How do we subtract sin? In Gal. 5:16, Paul says, "to live under the control of the Holy Spirit on a continuous basis and temptations will lessen."

4. **Deliverance of Crucifixion**. In Genesis 22, Abraham was asked to sacrifice what he loved and he received power to obey. When Abraham was about to sacrifice his son, God brought deliverance by stopping him and giving him a ram in a thicket. We must crucify that which we love and put Jesus first. When Jesus is first, He will give us joy, joy, joy!

Do You Have Your Keys?

Keys are used to gain access into locks. They give us a power of passage to freedom. Metaphorically, The Lord Jesus has all of the keys of both our physical and spiritual life. He has the keys to unlock us from bondage. He liberates our locks, and strengthens us in the midst of our struggles to enable us to overcome that which has over taken us. The Apostle Paul, in this context, will now approach the doctrine of sanctification. Sanctification means to be set apart. God wants to enable us, equip us and empower us to live a Godly life through sanctification. The true affect of whether the Holy Spirit is operating in your life is through sanctification. We have Victory, which is deliverance from the power of indwelling sin. Sin feels good, but it does not last.

1. **Curriculum: To Know** (Our Mind). There is knowledge associated with our victory. Our living has direct connection with our learning. Where there no learning there is no living, and where there is no doctrine there is no known duty. We are dead to sin. This is an act of God. We may not feel like it, but our feelings have nothing to do with this. We have options, we do not have to sin. We do not have to serve sin. The world is serving Satan, he has them trapped, but we are free from sin.

2. **Calculation: To Reckon** (Our Heart). To reckon means to impute, estimate, calculate in our imaginations, and to keep talking to ourselves. We must reckon oursleves to be dead to sin. This is not a feeling. We are dead to sin, but sin is not dead to us. When we feel like nothing is working, "hold on," keep believing Jesus and keep walking in His light.

3. **Commitment: To Yield** (Our Will). When we get saved we have two natures. We have the operation of the old, and the operation of the new. When Jesus died, He did something by way of operation to affect the outcome. We were crucified with Christ; The Holy Spirit cut away our old natures from our souls. Our soul is our means of existence and our personality. Christ has reattached it to our new nature. Now we should want to please Jesus instead of ourselves, walk in the newness of life and not participate in sin. If we are really saved, our desires have to change. We must yield to the Holy Spirit, which is an act of our wills. God has given us three aspects to yielding to the Holy Spirit:

1) **Favor**: Because of God's Grace, we do not want to sin.

2) **Freedom**: He has given us a governing freedom on the inside to choose Him over Satan, to choose righteousness over unrighteousness, and to choose deliverance over dirt.

3) **Fruit**: God gave us the keys to victory over sin.

We cannot be half-way Christians and be happy. We are either in or out. We will never have joy as long as there is junk in your life. Jesus has all the keys. Whatever man has, is because Jesus gave it to him. Only Jesus has the keys to Death, Hell and the Grave. Jesus has all Power. Do you have your keys?

Caterpillars are transformed into beautiful butterflies as they go through a series of rigorous changes. These changes are prompted by a purpose, a painful process, perseverance, and permanency. These changes take place from the inside out. The first area God performs surgery on, during a transformation, is the heart. Once we are saved, regenerated, and indwelt by the Holy Spirit, God begins to impact our hearts.

Before caterpillars are transformed into butterflies, they are hideous, hairy, and harmful to God's creation. It is through this period of transformation that caterpillars are metamorphosed. During this process its design, diet, and dependency changes. In a similar sense, when we become saved, our design, diet, and dependency should change. The definition of the heart is our imagination, thoughts, soul, personality, and emotions.

In the Old Testament, Hannah was speaking to God in her heart. We come to God with a wicked heart and He moves us through each stage from a breaking point to brokenness. Something must take place if our hearts are going to change; the soil must be plowed, the sower [God] must have pre-eminence, and the seed (Word of God) must be planted.

1. **The Putting Away of the Hard Heart** (Matthew 13:15). Hardhearted people are bothered, bruised, and bitter. They are negative about everything. They are hard because they say no to God concerning His direct will. Many are bothered because of a history that had something to do with church involvement. God wants to transform the hard-hearted. Let Jesus handle your bitterness.

2. **The Plowing of the Soft Heart** (Matthew 13:20-23). Softhearted people are going through a breaking process. They hear the Word, receive some of it, become happy, but allow trouble to destroy what they have learned. Satan has a strategy to snatch the Word from us and we do not realize that trouble helps us to grow. Difficulty will develop us. Softhearted people have a heart that is broken. God will break up our hearts. He will dig, develop, and divert the soil that must be treated by the Holy Spirit. He is hurting our hindrances, breaking out pride and pollution, and devastating our worldly desires.

3. **The Power and the Promise of a New Heart**. New-hearted people are broken. God is going to break our wills, our sin patterns, our stubbornness, and our bitterness. Everyone who met Jesus was broken. Paul, a persecutor, was broken while on his way to Damascus. God blinded him, broke his pride, and humbled him. Peter was a bragger. God broke him. He preached and many received the Gospel of Jesus Christ. God specializes in breaking us up.

After God breaks us, He wants praise for the trouble, triumph, and trials. He is able to do anything, but fail. He is going to transform us. We will be broken, molded, and yielded, which is His first line of transformation in changing our hearts because, out of the Heart are the issues of life.

The Process of Perfection

The Food and Drug Administration (FDA) has mandated that all food products produced in the U.S.A. bear labels on their containers listing all of the products and by products contained therein. The by products are a subtotal of the product within itself. The ingredients that are in by products help to make up the product. In a similar sense, our product is Salvation. Salvation is not an instant gift that is received when we come up the aisle in the church. It is a process that continues until we see Jesus. Many byproducts make up salvation.

1. **The Product of Reconciliation** (Colossians 1:15-23). Reconciliation takes place prior to being saved. It is a ministry of the Holy Spirit where God is drawing us to Himself. When God reconciles us, He presents us positionally faultless and blameless, in order to get us into a process where we will be transformed. We are new because of our position, not because of our walk. Our walk takes time to catch up with our position. God is in control of everything that deals with the process of salvation and reconciliation. It is not by our works, will, heritage, nor our histories; only God seeks and saves. Jesus causes us to become saved and then to change. What vehicle of reconciliation drew us to Christ? Was it deliberate, through difficulty, or was it a process of delay?

2. **The Product of Regeneration** (St. John 3:3-8). We cannot become saved until we hear the Truth (the Word of God), then the Holy Spirit will start to do His spiritual work through us. God now gives us His nature, and He changes our desires. Some of the by products of regeneration are sanctification (being set apart), and Son-ship (being adopted into the family of God). God takes us and places us into the Body of Christ, then Jesus places the Holy Sprit inside of us; this is called the sealing of the Holy Spirit. The Holy Spirit will never leave us until we see Jesus.

3. **The Product of Restoration** (Joel 2:25-26). If we live right, humble ourselves, and get in line with God, He will reverse the deadly process. He will turn our troubles into triumphs. He will restore the years that we have wasted in the world when Christ was not in our lives. He will bless us in spite of ourselves. God wants to restore our emotions, peace, joy, and wisdom, and give us back what we have lost. He will make us cry when others are not, shout when no one is around, and exalt His Name when

there is quietness in the room. He will restore the years that the locust have eaten.

4. **The Product of His Resume** (Colossians 1:17-18). God is the Preeminent One. He is Jehovah Jireh [The Lord our Provider], Jehovah Shalom [The Lord our Peace], Jehovah God [The self-existing One], Jehovah-El Rohi [He is my Shepherd], Jehovah Rophe [He is my Healer] and Jehovah-Tsidkenu [He is my Righteousness].

The Lord Jesus Christ died for our sins, He was buried in a tomb, but on the third day, He got up with all power in His hands. He is able to give us Light, Life, and Liberty. We cannot be transformed until we are saved, reconciled, regenerated, and restored. Jesus is worthy to be praised!

Stay Tuned for Station Identification

Every television network has specified times for commercials and station identification. The viewer must be reminded, while watching the program, of the program's sponsor. We can so easily get caught up in the program that we forget the one who is responsible for bringing the program to us. The spiritual parallel is that God, the Author and Finisher of our faith, has specified times to remind us that He is our Sponsor.

In this first chapter of the Book of 1 Timothy, Paul takes a station break to remind everyone that sound doctrine is the key to realizing the transforming power of the Holy Ghost in our lives. He identifies three major initiatives. First, He informs us that we have been translated from a troubled life into a triumphant life.

Secondly, we are made aware that the message of the Gospel transforms us from a sinful life to a sanctified life. Finally, we are told we have been transferred from a life that is empty to an exemplary life.

God is a change agent. He has a program that provides a pardon, and a process and a praise for His power. God has initiated a program in every Believer's life. The Gospel was promised in Genesis 3:15. The provision is outlined in St. John 3:16. The power is described in Romans 1: I6-17.

Paul begins to deal with the power of the gospel message:

1. **His Testimony**: Using his personal testimony, Paul sets out to persuade us of the power of the Gospel. The blind man in John 9, used his personal testimony to describe the power of Jesus Christ, "all I know; I was blind, but now I see." Paul, by using his personal testimony, wants us to pause for station identification. He wants to advertise for our great Sponsor. When was the last time we used our personal testimony to advertise the Power and Person of the Gospel?

2. **His Turbulent Past**: The turbulent past of Paul's life gives a clear picture of how the gospel translates us from trouble to triumph. In his past, he was a blasphemer (1 Tim.1:13). He denied the deity of the Lord Jesus Christ. Any religion or belief system that denies that Jesus is God is blasphemous. Paul was a violent bully determined to destroy anything or anyone associated with the Lord Jesus Christ. Paul was injurious,

consenting to have Stephen stoned. In spite of Paul's past, the Lord saved him not only from hell, but also saved him from a life of trouble, transforming him into a triumphant life.

3. **His Transformation**: A transition begins in 1 Tim.1:14, from Paul's translation to his transformation, Paul thought he was highly educated and intelligent, but he was blinded to the Truth. God caused mercy and grace to unite so that we could be saved and transformed. It is the goodness of the Lord that leads us to repentance. Paul describes the grace of the Lord as exceedingly abundant with faith and love. Paul experienced the pardon and went through the process. The power of the Gospel in Paul's life is demonstrated as he is transferred from a life of emptiness into a life of example (I Tim. 1:12). Paul went from being a persecutor to being a preacher. No longer a murderer, Paul became a missionary. Have you experienced God's pardon? He is the only one who can translate you out of hell and a life of trouble, into a life of triumph. Your life will no longer be empty; instead it will be an example.

When Visiting Hours Are Over

It is nice ot have visitors when they are expected, but when they are not expected, and no arrangements have been made for them, we tend to pout, panic, and become perplexed. There will be a series of visitations by unexpected visitors in life. Some visitors are problems from our past, consequences of our carnality, and troubles from God to transform us into the image of Jesus Christ. Other visitors are dysfunctions because of careless decisions, and some are to deflate our pride. Death, disease, sickness, and some things that are not welcome, will visit us. If we put our trust in Jesus Christ, when these things show up, grace will show up at the same time. Moses wrote the book of Genesis, and in the context of this Book, there are three critical tests that will be examined:

1. **Communion** (Gen.18): *There was a known guest* (communion with God). Today, people have translated fellowship and communion into having a good time. The question is, "Can Jesus come in for fellowship with us and not be offended?" Must we clean things out, first? Grievous sin brings God's judgment. God could not find ten people in Sodom, that were righteous. Today, we are living in the midst of a perverted, post-Christian society, and God is not pleased. It is a shame that the youth today are living in a society that is forced to make a decision based on how they feel about their sexuality. If we live right and do right, we will be able to put petitions before God and He will hear us. Prayers are not being answered because people are not in the will of God. We need communion with God.

2. **Condemnation** (Gen. 19): *There was an unwelcome guest.* Lot was saved, but soiled; connected, but carnal. We, the church, must deal with the subject of same-sex marriage. We are not gay bashers; We should not hurt nor harm people with verbal or physical abuse. Everyone has rights. But we need to know and do what the Bible says concerning sin. Society is being permeated and consumed with abhorent behavior and God is not pleased. When God gives us over to a reprobate mind, we are hell bound; there is no receiving salvation. We lose our fellowship, faith, and future. These lusts of the flesh are evil, and wicked. God will bring judgment on every person who is involved in homosexuality, and practicing bestiality. We cannot habitually practice sin, and be saved. We may fall into sin, but we must get up.

3. **Carnality** (Gen. 20): *There was an unpleasant guest.* The reason there is a repetition of our sin is because we have confessed the sin, but we have not judged the sin. When we judge the sin, we see it as God sees it. We say the same thing about the sin that God says. *Sin is you calling right wrong and wrong right.* We need to ask God to give us a hatred for sin.

Visiting hours are over. Soon and very soon, the Lord is coming back for a church without a spot or wrinkle. We must get our house in order!

FAMILY

Submitting yourselves one to another
in the fear of God.

Ephesians 5:21

Godly Fatherhood

Fatherhood is disappearing today from our society. Satan's objective has been to wreck the church and community by bringing deterioration to the <u>family</u>. Ninety percent of the men who are incarcerated have never had a real father. The father figure establishes a respect for authority in children and teaches them God's purpose for their lives. Fatherhood helps boys to aspire to be men, as they can see and touch a replica of God's blueprint. An earthly father prepares a child to trust and believe in a **Heavenly Father**.

Fatherhood also considerably helps little girls with special securities that they will need to interface with men in the future. A "godly father" lays a biblical foundation that equips little girls to interface and co-habit with the male gender.

Our first question should be, by definition, "What is a Godly father?" Before answering that question, We need to realize that there are hardly any in the Bible. Abraham was probably a good father in his later years; Moses was not a very good father; David, Eli and Solomon were not very good fathers either; Jacob and Isaac both showed favoritism, and Jacob was very scheming.

So the Bible does not really have a "Hall of Fame" for "godly fathers." I believe that our definition should come from a biblical job description of what "godly" fatherhood is all about. I believe that a "godly" father is identified by five positions:

1. **He is a Priest**:
   - ☐ He is the Priest of the family
   - ☐ He is a Priest that prays (Job 1)
   - ☐ He is a Priest that understands (Heb.10)
   - ☐ He is a Priest that teaches

2. **He is a Provider**:
   - ☐ He is a Provider (Matt.1:20-23)
   - ☐ He Provides a secure environment
   - ☐ He Provides a loving environment
   - ☐ He Provides a physically secure environment

3. **He is a Protector**:
   - ☐ He is the Protector
   - ☐ He emotionally Protects his family

   - ☐ He psychologically Protects his family
   - ☐ He physically Protects his family

4. **He is a Promoter**:
   - ☐ He is the primary Promoter
   - ☐ He Promotes unity (Joshua 24:1)
   - ☐ He Promotes training (Deu.6:4)
   - ☐ He Promotes discipline (Eph.6:4/ Col.3:21)

5. **He is a Politician**:
   - ☐ He is a Politician
   - ☐ He Polices the home environment

   - ☐ He Polices the thinking and maturity process of the children

A Celebration for a Celebrity

All mothers, whether single, married, or divorced, should be applauded for their sacrificial love. If married, she should also be applauded for giving to her husband, her management skills, as well as her manifold wisdom. In the context of the Bible, we find that Hannah [1 Samuel], was a mother of prayer and preparation. Lois and Eunice [mother and grandmother] prioritized for young Timothy. They feared and had faith in the Lord. Mary, the mother of Jesus, pondered with a deep and internal reflection, about what God had said to her about His unique Son. She did not understand what God was doing and the uniqueness of the Son that she had birthed. How could she raise God?

The virtuous woman is unnamed because she was not a specific person, she is a paradigm. The Bible paints this picture to show what Godly women, who fear the Lord, should be. She personifies wisdom and not worldliness; her specialties are her inner beauty, business, and benefit to others. Her value is her character. She compliments everyone around her. *This woman is not found; she is framed by God.* The Holy Spirit produces her. Proverbs 31 asks, "who can find a virtuous woman?"

1. **Godly Fear** (Prov. 31:10-12). Her priority is to protect her home. Her mission is to promote her husband with whom she is not fighting or competing. Her husband is safe because he does not feel threatened by her outside activities or attentions. Her mission does not start with the children, but with her husband. Her motive is to protect her children from her personal, historical, and life suffering issues. However, a woman with no wisdom tears down her own husband by competing with him, continually criticising him, comparing him with other men, and constantly confronting him. She tears down what God wants to bless.

2. **Godly Fruit** (Prov. 31:13-20). The virtuous woman always seeks ways to safeguard the home. She manages the resources. She supplies whatever is needed with her wise investment. Raising our children is not always going to be a happy endeavor. There will be struggles in the marriage, with the kids and within us. Mothers have to handle all of this, even when the fathers get lazy, idle, and turn their heads away from what needs attention. She also has a ministry outside the home; she helps others.

3. **Godly Fashion** (Prov. 31:25-31). She wears strength and honor because she is a lady. She opens her mouth with wisdom. Her words are kind. She is constantly aware of what is needed for the home. Her children rise up and call her blessed, and her husband also, as he praises her. It is not enough to have beauty on the outside and be a failure on the inside. The beauty that God is talking about is the fruit of the Holy Spirit, which is love, joy, peace, longsuffering, kindness, wisdom, and godliness. This woman is rare, righteous, respected, refreshing, responsible, and redeemed. We celebrate her as a celebrity. She is endowed with Godly wisdom. She resembles Jesus Christ. This virtuous woman is a model to emulate, through the power of the Holy Spirit.

A Coach in Crisis

Fatherhood is a highly critical component to the life and liberation of a child. Fatherhood is a picture of God, a portrait of grace and growth, and a paradise of goodness. Fathers are facilitators who later become friends and are constantly encouraging. They are responsible for discipline and are dedicated to the development of their children. A father must be a coach. He must know how to teach, must have a game plan, and at times may have to bench a player that can not carry-out instructions. There are three areas that must be enforced in any relationship; rules, respect, and responsibilities. A father's role is to initiate a four-fold equipping for their children.

1. **The Expectation of a Father**: He must provide goods for his household, which means he must have a job. He must provide emotional security, encouragement, and protect his household from any threats that will come into their lives. In Deuteronomy 6, the Lord told His people that He would prepare and instruct them in the things of the Lord, and bring them to a place of maturity. Just as God the Father did the instructing then, fathers must do the instructing of their children now. The father is the priest of the home. Fathers should lead their family in prayer.

2. **The Education of a Father**: Fathers must teach issues of life to their children, how to control their desires and pleasures. They need to know how to control their appetite in this sick sexual world. They should teach temperance, tolerance, and how to handle turmoil. Fathers should instruct their children how to be a good leader; not a follower in the community.

3. **The Expression of a Father**: Fathers should teach their children to respect elders. All children need affirmation, even if they do not always meet the mark of success. They need to know that we are pleased with what they are trying to accomplish. Girls need to have their first date with their fathers. Girls need closeness from their fathers and boys need hugs from their fathers. Additionally, children must be taught how to budget their money, how to act on a date, what to expect when their hormones start to over-react.

4. **The Example of a Good-Father**: In Luke 15, the lost son was released by the father into the Lord's hand. This is not always easy to do. We need not always run to rescue our children. Let

them learn lessons the hard way. When we continually rescue the rebellious, they will become more resistant. They must face the hard knocks of life. It will not hurt them as much as it will help them. The releasing of a child is love. Give them to Jesus. Sometimes they need to get in a place, especially if they are rebellious, where you will not help them out. This is needed in order for them to come to their senses. Furthermore, fathers need to forgive their children when they make mistakes, especially your older children. Learn to say, "I'm sorry". We have all made mistakes. Fathers must reward their children when they come to their senses. We need fathers, not Cool Daddy's. We need to cover all angles of our child's life, from the cradle to the grave. Help them, don't hinder them.

Do You Have A Game Plan?

Fatherhood is a tough task. It involves instructing children in righteousness, respect, and responsibility, with the intent to release them. A father must be a coach, caretaker, comforter and a cheerleader. The father is the glory of his children. The father often forms a child's initial concept of our heavenly Father. His role is to provide instruction about the divine Person of Jesus Christ, about the discernment needed for life, the duties of life, and the discipling and preparation of his children for departure.

There are five major areas in which fathers must instruct their children:

1. **The Divine Person of Jesus Christ:** Fathers need to establish in the minds and hearts of their children that there is only one true and living God. "That thou mightest fear the Lord thy God, to keep all his statutes and his commandments which I command thee, thou, and thy son and thy son's son, all the days of thy life..." (Deut. 6:2). The father's role as instructor must be practiced with diligence. Fathers must be active. If a father is passive, he cannot expect to raise healthy children. Children should learn to worship God with passion. They must learn to worship the Lord in spirit and truth. Fathers are to teach their children to "love the Lord with all their heart, soul, and might" (V.5). His instruction not only involves the Person and the Passion of Christ, but also includes precaution. He is to warn his children not to forget God (V.12).

2. **Discernment:** Children need to be taught discernment by their fathers. They need to know how to think, observe and make decisions based upon God's Word. Children need to be able to exercise discernment in the pathways and provisions of life. Fearing God in their decisions and honoring God with their provisions will ensure spiritual success (Prov. 3:7,9). Children are taught discernment through correction. They need to learn to be at peace with correction.

3. **Duties:** Instruction in life includes teaching children to be responsible in their duties. They need to know how to exercise wisdom, recognize wickedness, and be wise about women and men. Fathers must teach their children about God's view of sex. Three chapters in the Book of Proverbs include instruction about

the dangers of the strange woman. Children need to understand the value of their virginity, and the emotional, psychological and spiritual consequences of pre-marital sex.

4. **Discipleship**: Fathers must intentionally disciple their children. There are three critical things every father needs to provide: unconditional love, belief in their children, and discipline. Therefore, children have great difficulty forgiving a parent who fails to discipline. "Whom the Lord loves he chastens" (Heb. 12:6).

5. **Departure**: Children have to be instructed in preparation for their departure. David, near death, gives instruction to Solomon in work, wisdom and walk. He exhorts him to do the work of a man (I Kings 2:2). Teach children to be responsible for their decisions. Privilege must always be balanced by responsibility.

Fathers, do you have a game plan? God has a plan for us. He coaches, cares, and comforts us. Are we coaching, caring for, and comforting our children?

Eliminating Our Excuses

Paralysis is a debilitating handicap that restricts movement and function. In a similar sense, the family is traumatized by its hurts, wounds, and wills. Our parenting, our partnership, and our peace are cracked and fractured because we don't spiritually understand the impact that our past is having on our present. Yet, once we confess what we are and who we are, God says He is faithful and He is just, not only to forgive, but to keep on cleansing us from all unrighteousness (I John 1:9). In John chapter 5, Jesus asks the paralytic, "Do you want to be healed." The man makes excuses. Nevertheless, Jesus tells the man to get up, pick up his bed, and walk. In other words, whatever excuse we use, we need to take it up today, put it on our shoulders, and move on. There are three important reasons why we are paralyzed:

1. **We Need Healing from the Paralysis of our Parenting**. Children need affection; we cannot allow our issues to prevent us from hugging our kids. Children need affirmation; we need to compliment them. If we criticize more than compliment, we are messing them up. Children need advice; Thus, whatever we don't tell our kids, the world will. We need to give advice on the company they keep, their careers, and their decisions. Children need us to withdraw our anger. When fathers remain angry with their children, children give up. For our adult children who live at home, we need to help them fix their problems, we need to help them facilitate their decisions, and we need to help them to become free and independent.

2. **We Need Healing from the Paralysis of our Partnerships**. Instead of commitment, we entered into our partnership for convenience. Biblical love is giving and committing without expecting anything in return. There also needs to be a passion and a pleasing of our mate. Col. 3:8-14 tells us to put off anger, wrath, malice, blasphemy, and filthy communication out of our mouths. We need to put on the new man; only then can we put on love. The main problem in our relationships is a lack of intimacy. Intimacy does not merely come from a sexual relationship. Intimacy is full disclosure of both partners. It is predicated in Phil. 3:8, which states that we must be willing to take all our assets and count them as garbage just to get into an intimate relationship with Jesus. If we are intimate with Christ, it will free us to be intimate with our spouse. When we are not

intimate with our spouse the devil moves in with a lie. Intimacy begins with trusting Jesus and an act of the will.

3. **We Need Healing from the Paralysis of our Lack of Peace.** The peace of God only comes when there is a spirit of mercy, kindness, humbleness of mind, meekness, longsuffering, forbearance and forgiveness (Col. 3:12b-13). Then we can let God rule in our hearts. This means we need to let go of our controls, let go of our way of thinking, and let go of the historical mess we keep conjuring up.

Let God fix our fractures, our minds, our wills, our walk, and our talk because He is ". . . able to do exceeding abundantly above all that we ask or think..." (Eph. 3:20). Jesus told the paralyzed man to get up, take up his bed and walk. We must get up and walk to eliminate the excuses!

A Loving Liberator

Mothers are God's tools of Love and Grace. They are instruments in partnership and passion, with the husband's preparation of their children. They have protection in the context of promoting their families. When children are growing up, they are more attached to their mothers than to their fathers. The hand that rocks the cradle really controls the nation. Nevertheless, there are too many women concentrating more on exercising their spiritual gifts outside of the home, when their attention should be to their household. What constitutes a Godly mother?

1. **A Mother's Commitment** (Manager): A mother causes her house to flourish. A wise woman builds her house with love. Children need affirmation and love. Thus, she must be careful with the words that are spoken in her house, especially about her children. She understands her place in the home as a manager. Satan has devalued the mother's role. He has relegated the job of a mother to a place beneath all other jobs. God calls a mother a helpmeet, and defines her role as managnig the home for her husband.

2. **A Mother's Counsel** (Mentor): A mother teaches her children about holiness, sobriety, and compassion. She must teach her children about the dangers of drugs and wrong company. She cannot allow her children to put guilt complexes on her. She should be able to create the rules for her household. This does not mean that her children will not go astray. There is no guarantee that her children will not fall, but she does her part to instruct them in a Godly manner. We as parents have made mistakes, but it is God's will for mother's to get help for whatever issues her children have. A mother should influence and embrace her children.

3. **A Mother's Care** (Manufacturer): "Who can find a virtuous woman"? She can't be found. God can only manufacture her. A virtuous woman is one who spends time with the Lord, fears the Lord, and walks with the Lord. She is a treasure of trust and a treasure to her husband. Her husband comes before her children. She compliments and does not compete with her husband. She is a treasure to her household. Her children call her blessed, and her husband praises her also. A mother must know what God has called her to do.

A woman that fears the Lord shall be praised. God has not forgotten her labor of love, and He is on her side. A mother is God's tool, and He has blessed her with grace and strength to perform her positional duties. Mother's will never get enough praise, concentration, and affirmation. Mothers, look to Jesus for your encouragement!

The Majesty of a Mother's Praise

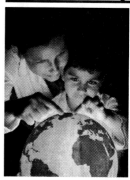

A Godly mother is a compliment to her husband, a coordinator in her home, and a comfort to her children. A mother's love helps to liberate and to affirm her children. A mother's support helps to lighten the load of her husband, and a mother's prayer helps to prepare her children for life. If ever there was a formula of facilitating a family and a pathway to a productive life, it is recorded in the life of Hannah, in 1 Samuel. Hannah was a praying mother. She also prepared, persevered, and praised the Name of Yahweh.

There is, in the text about Hannah, a fourfold initiative of prayer:

1. **Hannah's Conflict of Prayer.** Hannah prayed through her conflict. The providence of God caused her pain - she could not bear children. There are four premises to prayer in the Bible. First is the prayer of praise. Second is the pattern of prayer (Matthew 6; and Luke 11). Jesus taught His disciples to pray. The prayer had to do with worship and the will of God. Third is the prayer for our petitions. Fourth, there is praying through our pain. In Gethsemane, Jesus prayed that the cup of the wrath of God would pass. Then He prayed God's Will to be done. Hannah's prayer was one of pain. She was childless and criticized, yet she prayed through the providence of God. Mothers must teach their children to pray through pain, because life brings pain.

2. **Hannah's Commitment to Prayer.** Hannah, in her bitterness of soul, prayed to the Lord. In 1 Samuel 1:11, Hannah cried out to the Lord, "Remember me!" There are times when we are so overthrown by trials that we can only pray, "Lord, remember me!" It was a prayer of trust, not trying; It was a prayer of dependence; not independence. Hannah prayed through her pain. She depended on the grace of God (V.18). She continued to pray through her plight.

3. **Hannah's Confidence in Prayer.** When we pray, we must believe. Hannah's confidence in prayer was shown by her ability to walk away and believe (V.18). She believed God would honor her and move on her behalf. We must pray believing that God will answer our prayers.

4. **Hannah's Celebration of Prayer.** In 1 Samuel chapter 2, Hannah praised God after He gave her the baby. First, Hannah disclosed her heart. Her heart rejoiced (2:1a). God wants us

to commit our requests to Him and then rejoice as though He has already answered the prayer. Second, she disclosed her horn (her power) in 2:1b. Her power was in the Lord. Third, she dealt with God's Holiness (V.2). She praised God for His Holiness. Fourth, she humbled herself. God honors humility (vv.3-5). God hates pride. He wants us to humble ourselves under His almighty hand. In verses 4-9, Hannah disclosed her hope. She knew God was able to reverse the situation. God is able to bless us when we think we are buried.

Lastly, Hannah declared her happiness (vv.20-26). Hannah trusted God and fulfilled her vow by bringing Samuel to God. Hannah teaches us that mothers ought to pray. Mary, the mother of Jesus, was a pondering mother. Lois and Eunice were preparing mothers. Jachobed, mother of Moses, was a performing mother. The virtuous woman was a prototypical mother!

Marriage

Is it a Contract or Covenant?

In baseball, before a game begins, the umpires, coaches, and team captains meet at home plate to exchange line-up cards, and establish the ground rules. The purpose of the line-up cards is to ensure that everybody in the stadium knows who is going to play, and to establish boundaries of play before the game begins. At a wedding, the Holy Ghost, the preacher, and the bride and groom exchange their line-up cards. During the exchange of vows, ground rules are established. These rules are not established by contract; a contract is an agreement or pledge between two or more parties. A covenant carries a far greater obligation. The word covenant comes from the Old Testament Hebrew word "Berith," which signifies three different types of legal relationships.

☐ Berith may mean a two-sided covenant between known parties, both of which voluntarily accept the terms of the agreement. This type of covenant includes the covenant of friendship (I Samuel 18, between David and Jonathon), and a political covenant found in Joshua 9:15.

☐ Berith can mean a one-sided disposition imposed by a superior party, as in Ephesians 5:17. The Lord commands Berith while man, the servant, is to obey.

☐ Berith can mean God's self imposed obligation for the reconciliation of sinners to Himself (Deut. 7 and Ps. 89). He stated to Abraham, "I will establish my (Berith) covenant between me and thee."

Biblical marriage stems from a covenant (Berith) between two parties who voluntarily agree to its terms. The purpose of God's covenant of marriage is a proposal for a framework to a fruitful family. Its primary ingredients are: Partnership (Genesis 2:20; 3:12; I Corinthians 11:9), Procreation (Genesis 1:28), Passion (Hebrews 13:4 – Honorable and Pleasurable), and Purity (Genesis 2:25; I Corinthians 7:2-9). The provisions of God's covenant of marriage, are found in Eph. 5:1-23. Not only is the purpose of marriage a partnership for procreation, pleasure, and purity, but marriage is also a picture of Christ's relationship to the Church. God made a Berith in Heaven. It was not a two-sided covenant between known parties who voluntarily accepted the terms, but was a self-imposed obligation for the reconciliation of sinners to Himself. The blood was shed so that God could unconditionally save us freely because a Berith had been established (Heb. 10). "For by one offering He hath perfected forever them that are sanctified." God met with God before the foundation of the world, and He (Berithed) covenanted with Himself that He would snatch us out of hell and save us, transform us, and seat us in heavenly places in Christ Jesus.

Thank God we have a covenant and not a contract. If we had signed a contract, we would have breached that contract the moment we signed it. We would have broken it with ungodly words, immoral sins, ungodly attitudes. **Remember, Marriage is a covenant with God!**

RELATIONSHIPS

Be kindly affectioned one to another
with brotherly love; in honour preferring
one another.

Romans 12:10

Biblical Relationships

Relationships become difficult when its' participants lack the discerning of Biblical information. Some of this information must be taught from a Biblical context regarding roles, rules, and responsibilities of the people involved. A marriage only works when two people are committed to a cause, a covenant and a curriculum. The cause is God's will, the covenant is God's wisdom, and the curriculum is God's watchfulness. Marrital relationships should establish a covenant, composed of five critical areas:

1st – **Faithfulness**: One's total commitment unto another; a comprehensive, clear concept of one's faithfulness to one another.

2nd – **Forever**: One's timeless commitment unto another, for time does not affect the covenant. Time should neither change nor conclude it; it is until death do us part, and is conditionless.

3rd – **Faith**: We must have faith in God, through Jesus Christ, to be a mediator within our relationship. We must trust the Lord, and exercise biblical faith in the keeping, counseling, and custodianship of the marriage. We must also allow the Bible, the Word of God, to governs our affairs.

4th – **Forgiveness**: We should exercise forgiveness as a healing to our troubles. Forgiveness must be initiated in our love and communication with each other.

5th – **Facilitation**: One's roles/rules and responsibilities. We should enter into a covenant agreement with this understanding. This would include being accountable to one another. We should agree to fully accept one another, be accountable to one another's feelings, and try desperately not to become angry, yet, set boundaries in our relationships.

Couples, have we ever thought about this?

• Men ought to study their spouse.

• How do we spiritually fight temptation?

• How are we honest with ourselves and our spouses?

• Do we examine our ungodly attitudes (arrogance, control, pride & bitterness)?

- What do we do when in-laws become outlaws?
- How do we prevent infidelity? – Learn to recognize the signs.
- Are we speaking one another's love language?
- Are we giving what women need in a marriage: honesty, respect, affection, romance, esteem and trust?
- Are we giving what a man needs in a marriage: respect, sex, appreciation, trust, and patience?
- Are our needs being met: psychologically, emotionally and sexually?
- Do we really listen with an ear of love?
- Are we complementing our mate?
- Men, are we a provider?
- Men, we can help with the chores, run her a bubble bath and give her a massage.
- Women, you can surprise him with a candlelight dinner and watch the game with him.

Phonies Don't Function

Relationships require three significant ingredients: sacrifice, service, and personal submission or surrendering of one's rights. Romans 12:1-2 teaches us that our relationship with God had to be met with sacrifice of dedication, where we present our bodies as an act of worship. We are not to be conformed to the world, (outward pressure) but transformed (inward power) by the renewing of our minds. In verses 3-8 the emphasis changes to other believers in the Body of Christ and the requirement is service.

As we begin to look at self-denial and a planned surrender to what is good for the other person, we need to ask ourselves, "how do we function as born again Believers in the Body of Jesus Christ?" The answer is, "phonies don't function."

All relationships require sacrifice, service, and a personal surrender. Many relationships don't work because we are egocentric. We are in a "me first" world, where our needs are not being met and we want out! Relationships will not always make us feel good. All of your needs will not be met, and you will not always be happy. Relationships are for mature people with the ability to give without expecting anything. When couples first get married they only see glitter. After the glitter comes the grind, then growth, and then glory.

There will be a grind in every relationship; this is what many do not want to deal with. Many times people will not get what they desire because they cannot handle it. If He gives us everything we desire, it will bring damage to ourselves and to others. Whatever God entrusts into our hands, He makes sure we have the grace to handle it. Power can divert you, but there has to be humility. There is nothing great about us. We must keep telling ourselves that we are nothing. Everything that we have today is only by God's Grace. Our gifts are not for our egos, but for edification. Pride can get in the way when God gives us something, but only God must get the Glory. There are three areas in which Christians must function:

1. **Sacrificial Mindset** (Rom. 12:3): We must fight the desire to become great in our own eyesight. We must become broken before we can help others. If we do not, God will harness us, to keep us under His control. He will usually leave something in our lives to make us pray and depend on Him. When we spend

time with Jesus, He will break us, make us, and shape us in His love. Then, whatever God asks of us, we can do with a humble mindset.

2. **Service to the Membership** (Rom. 12:4-5): We are to be unified, but not uniformed. We are to operate with the same mindset because of what and who we believe; however, we do not all dress alike. God never asked us to look alike, but He did ask us to think alike. We have many members in our body, but one body in Christ. There are no denominations mentioned in the Bible. Oftentimes, we separate ourselves from one another, but this is not God's design. We are to serve one another in love.

3. **Service in Ministry** (Rom. 12:6-8): God has given us speaking, serving, and sign gifts. We must never try to exercise our gifts over the measure of faith that God has connected with the gift. God will do what He wants and we must not take credit for what He does through us. We are all servants for God. Phonies don't function: they pout, play, pretend, and preempt. We must serve each other and bring Glory to God. Everyone should want to participate, be excited, witness to the lost, work in the church, pray, become humble, and get in the place where Jesus can use you.

A Slow Leak

Anyone who drives a car and has experienced a slow leak in their tires is familiar with the false hope that they do not have a problem. Slow leaks are disheartening because the tire appears to be okay, but the leak is not detectable until it's too late. In the same sense, our homes are being attacked by a barrage from Satan. Desires are replacing duty, faith has been replaced by feelings, volition has replaced marriage vows, and lust has replaced love. The church is silent because we are more concerned with prosperity  and supernatural healing than we are in helping the institutions God has created. Why are we under such pressure in our relationships? The answer is four-fold:

1. **The Slow Leak of a False Hope**. One of the devil's deceptive devices is to fill us with unrealistic expectations. There are three misconceptions which give us a false sense of hope. First, there is a misconception of love. Love is an acceptance of another person. Until we accept that person, we will have problems. Love releases anger. It is willing to forgive as Christ forgave us. Love helps us to adapt to the one to whom we are married. Secondly, there is a misconception of liberation. Solomon teaches us about the quest for pleasure without God's principles. It leads to emptiness. Marriage will not liberate us nor make us feel good about ourselves. Thirdly, there is a misconception about loneliness. People who marry because they are lonely are treading on dangerous ground. Unless we are satisfied with Jesus first, we will not feel loved, be liberated, or be able to deal with the loneliness.

2. **The Slow Leak of a Fractured History**. All of us are hostages of our past. First, we have dysfunctions due to the past. This means that some of our thinking mechanisms are not in proper order. But, when we get married and have children, we should become the least important. Our marriage and our children must come before us. We must raise our kids in a climate of security, even though we may want to give up. We must sacrifice our feelings for our family. Secondly, there is dissatisfaction. Some of us are dissatisfied because we feel like victims. We are not victims. Thirdly, there is devastation. We hold each other hostage and fight the wrong person due to past devastation. The one we now hold hostage is not the one who devastated

us. What we do because of our past devastation will affect our children in their futures.

3. **A Fictional Happiness.** Many people are looking for a fictional happiness. We have turned from commitment to compatibility. The only One who can give us happiness is Jesus.

4. **A Failed Hermeneutic.** The Bible says that if a man finds a wife, he finds a good thing. Relationships require work, wisdom, and a covering of wounds. The work is a process that leads to maturity. There must be agreement on roles (who will do what), rules for the relationship, respect in the relationship, and raising the kids. Men must provide for the family. Love will not pay bills, keep the heat on, or provide the tithe. Additionally, there must be a covering of our wounds. When we marry someone, they also have wounds. Are we willing to cover them?

According to scripture, marriage is a model of the Church and Christ. Christ loved and served the church sacrificially. He did not divorce us when we sinned against Him. He forgave us of our sin and restored us.

The Bible says we have a slow leak, a false hope, a fractured history, a fictional happiness, and a failing hermeneutic because we do not know how to follow its instructions. The Bible says that we must cover one another, sacrifice for one another, serve one another, pray for one another, and lift one another up. Relationships will cost us something. "If any man will come after me, he must take up his cross and follow Me."

SPIRITUAL GROWTH

But grow in grace, and in the knowledge

of our Lord and Saviour Jesus Christ.

To Him be glory both now and for ever.

2 Peter 3:18

Growing Pains

When an infant begins to grow, he/she will experience growing pains. A child must pass through these natural stages if he is to mature properly. God's purpose is for us to grow into the image of His Son, Jesus Christ. It is expedient that we become mature in Christ so that we can live lives of power and peace. Just as a baby drools when it is developing teeth, falls when it is beginning to walk, and babbles when it is trying to talk, we must be exposed to some unavoidable pain. These growing pains can depress us when we think we are at one level and find out that we are at another level. These pains can at times dislodge us as we begin to struggle with our sanctification. Yet, there is a major four-fold design by God for the born again believer to grow up:

1. **Spiritual Growth Requires Doctrinal Learning**. We need a daily diet of God's Word, not just a Sunday feeding. 2 Tim. 3:16 tells us that the Bible is God breathed. The mechanism is through instruction and the maturing factor is by way of doctrinal learning. We must adjust our schedule to spend time learning the Word, if we are to grow.

2. **Spiritual Growth Requires Devotional Leaning**. We need a time of meditation-- a practice of pondering the truth of the Word. In this way, God starts building up a reservoir on the inside. The Holy Spirit gives us strength to be able to withstand the attacks of the enemy. This is done through prayer, devotions, and by putting on the armor of God, daily. Furthermore, in Phil. 4:8, Paul tells us what we should be thinking about whatever is true, just, right, pure, clean, undefiled, etc. When we think on these things, we can enjoy peace.

3. **Spiritual Growth Requires a Designed Leaving**. We must leave something in order to follow Jesus. Christians who try to follow and carry the world with them are crushed. When this happens, God may choose a yoke such as problems with our children, our marriage, or our finances to cause us to walk closer with Him. In Eph. 4:22, Paul tells us to put off the former life. Then, we must put on the new man (V.24). We cannot continue in the way we used to be. What we know about God ought to affect our actions. When we do not do what we know the Spirit wants us to do, we grieve Him (V.30).

4. **Spiritual Growth Requires Delightful Living**. Phil. 3:10 tells

us how we come to know Jesus. We know Jesus when all hell is breaking out and He is on-board. In verses 13-14, Paul tells us to forget what is behind. Whatever happened yesterday should be left to yesterday. When we do this, the promise is a peace that guards our mind and heart.

The more we grow in grace, the less things bother us. Once we know that He is able, He can turn a furnace into a fellowship, our trials into triumphs, and our pouting into praise. For this to happen we must grow!

Blessings on the Back-End

God's foresight is so great that He has engineered blessings into our lives that will emerge on the back-end. This is illustrated in the way almost every child receives chastening from their parents. Our parents gave us whippings for wisdom, punishment for purity, and discipling for development. Our parent's objective was not to hurt us, but to help us. There was a design to their discipline. God's disciplinary mode ultimately leads to our deliverance.

We are not to despise the chastening of the Lord. When we are going through difficulties, the temptation is to think God does not love us or have our best interest at heart. If we begin to despise the difficulty, not understanding that there is an all wise God overseeing everything, we will become depressed and start pulling away from the Word and the wisdom of Almighty God.

In the text of Hebrews 12, there is a three-fold significance to God's discipline:

1. **The Reasons for Our Discipline**. Discipline is to prompt a remembrance (V.5).The reason we chasten our children is so they will not forget. God also prompts us to remembrance. When we are going through difficulties, we forget the goodness of God. Therefore, God chastens us so we do not forget. Discipline proves God's love for us. Verse 5b says, my son, do not despise the chastening (instruction in right behavior), of the Lord. God's tool for chastening can be sickness, financial difficulty, a lack of peace, etc. God's method motivates us to right behavior. Satan wants us to believe the difficulties of life are because God does not love us. We must thank God in, not for, the circumstances; this is an act of faith. By thanking Him we are saying to God that He is all wise, all powerful, and in control. The result is peace. God uses discipline to turn our direction back to holiness. In verse 9, we see the pattern of discipline. We give fathers credit for their imperfect chastening. Should we not give credit to the heavenly Father who gives us discipline? His discipline results in an abundant life of joy.

2. **The Reactions to Our Discipline**. When we are being chastened, we have one of three attitudes: First, the Believer can despise it or treat it too lightly and not learn from it. Second, the Believer can faint under it. We may consider the discipline

as too much to bear. Third, the Believer can learn how to straighten himself out because of the discipline.

3. **The Results of Our Discipline**. We are told that chastening produces the peaceable fruits of righteousness (v. 11). What are the benefits of being chastened by God? First, there is a discontinuance of sin. Second, God gives us a new desire to strive to do what is right. Third, God gives us peace in our lives. God, through correction, sets us up for blessings. He is putting us in the right place at the right time for the right reward. Because of our correction, repentance and praise, He blesses us, He comforts us, and He brings us back. He makes us stand up. He gives us strength, power, and joy on the back-end.

Critical Closure

Closures in the faith are much more fearful than those found in fairy tales. Only characters in fairy tales live happily ever after. Closures in Christ are a continuous ministry of critical commitment to correct the wrongs of God's people. It is to counsel, to confront, and hopefully to conform them to the Word of God. Our closures are a continual warfare. Our labor and work is to be faithful, fruitful, fearless, and fundamentally sound in doctrine. When we look at the whole scope of Christianity, God never promised that we would go out happily.

Throughout the Christian life, we must participate in worship and warfare, study and standing still, praying and practicing truth, fighting and exercising faith. This life is a continuous commitment to carry out the will, the way, and the Word of Almighty God. False preachers who preach prosperity, healing, and a happy life have deceived too many Christians.

The Bible speaks of a commitment to a cause and to the Lord Jesus Christ. God has placed something in us, which will help prepare us for the work that He has for us to do. Moses was a man of fear, failure, and frustration. God used that in him, to deal with rebellious people. Paul was reminded of his pain every time he witnessed to people. Our pain will not always go away. Nehemiah spent 12 hard years of traveling, rebuilding, and fighting. He returned only to find out the people fell back into sin, yet, he was ready to correct, counsel and confront. There were five aspects to Nehemiah's confrontation:

1. **He Reflects on their Separation.** There was a threat to their sanctification. We should become transformed and conformed to the Word of God. We must fight to remain pure.

2. **He Reminds them of their Biblical Reform.** There was a threat to their support system. We need to deal with God's provisions to get His work done.

3. **He Rebukes them because of their Threat to the Sabbath.** This deals with the program of God. His program should not be altered. The Church is under a major attack.

4. **He Reacts to a Threat of their Solidarity.** We should have a passion for the purposes of God. We must learn to adapt to whatever life gives out, knowing that Jesus is on our side. Stop

fooling yourself about life. Job tells us that life is short and full of trouble. Suffering is a part of life.

5. **He Rejoices in the Results of God's Sovereignty**. Instead of pouting, we need to say, "Lord, I may not know why or what you are doing in my life, but, I know you are working things out for my good and Your glory."

What is going to represent the dash (-) between the date you were born and the date of your death? Something should glorify Jesus Christ. We should be committed to a Critical Closure; serving the Lord until the day we die. We want to hear Jesus say, "Well done, thy good and faithful servant. Thou has been faithful over a few things, I will make you ruler over many." (Mt. 25:21-23)

Cut the Cord

There is a unique connection between mother and child from the moment of conception. That connection is critical while the child is yet in the mother's womb. However, once the child is born, the umbilical cord is cut to separate the child from its mother. The child begins its separate life outside of the womb. In a similar sense, when we are truly born again, the Holy Spirit begins to separate us from the dependence upon the flesh and the world. It is critical that we sit under a rightly divided Word to walk in truth. We must not be caught up in the strategies of the age; nor should we fall prey to bad doctrine. John lays out the walk of a transformed life, which will result in tranquility; but this takes work and pain. As we go through suffering, our view of our suffering will make us bitter or better; pout or shout; groan or grow. We have to know Jesus signed off on everything that comes into our lives. John gives us three factors for cutting our umbilical cord to the world.

1. **What Leads to Transformation** (1 John 5:1-5): The one who has saving faith has taken the first step toward being an overcomer of the world. Saving faith is permanency and commitment because it will take us through frictions, failures, falls, and frustrations. This type of faith automatically engineers, within the believer, an outworking of love (V.1). Faith produces an outworking of obedience to His commands (V.3). Finally, faith produces victory that helps us to overcome (V.4). We will be victorious in our Christian life because He has predestined us to be conformed to His image. When we are saved, we still have two natures, old and new. The old nature is still attracted to the sins of the world; warring between the two natures is why Christians are in so much turmoil. It takes time to learn how to yield to the new nature. It is the Holy Spirit's job to conform us. We cannot do it ourselves, nor can we make others do it. It is through Christ's enablement that we overcome by faith.

2. **Witness of Truth** (1 John 5:6-13): John speaks of three witnesses. First, at Christ's baptism, the Father testified that Jesus was His Son. Secondly, when Christ died there was a supernatural darkness, an earthquake, and a ripping of the veil of the temple. Some external witnesses are water and blood. The third witness is the Holy Spirit, the Spirit of Truth is an internal witness.

3. **Will that Leads to Tranquility** (1 John 5:14-21): God sends us confidence to do His will. Lot got in trouble because he

made wrong decisions based on his own reasoning. This God given assurance involves the overthrowing of the enemy. John names five assurances for those who live in the will of God. (1) We know that we have eternal life (V.13). (2) We have answered prayer (V.14) because we pray according to His will and He will hear us (V.15). (3) We are tranquil because we love. (4) We will keep His commandments. (5) We will hear the internal witnesses.

God gives us life, love, liberty, truth and tranquility because, "greater is He that is in you than he that is in the world." God makes the difference, but we must Cut the Cord connecting us to the world, if we want to follow Him.

Don't Move into a Mishap

Whenever there is movement by man in the Word of God, it is either a device of God or a deception of Satan. We are being led or lied to; encouraged or entrapped; directed or detoured. Adam and Eve moved from God's place and purposes to pleasure. On the other hand, Abraham moved from his pleasures to God's place and purposes. Moses moved from luxury to liability. Joseph moved from the pit, to a prison to a palace.

In Acts 20:22-24, Paul is speaking to the elders in Ephesus in a farewell message. Paul has been faithful to Jesus and he wants them to be faithful also. In verses 18-21, he deals with the future. Paul tells them that after he leaves, wolves will come in to try to devour the flock. Therefore, he wants them to be on guard, (vv.28-38). Finally, Paul deals with the present, (vv.22-27). The four virgin daughters of Philip the evangelist, as well as the prophet Agabus, warn Paul not to return to Jerusalem, but Paul's response is that he will go. Subsequently, when he comes into Jerusalem, Paul is locked up, shipped to Rome, placed before a judge, and becomes a prisoner. This means that he could not take the Gospel where he wanted it to go. When we are warned by God not to move, and we move anyway, there will be consequences.

Paul describes his situation through metaphors from verses 22-25. The first metaphor shows Paul as an accountant. Paul examines his assets and his liabilities and decides to put Jesus first (V.22). The next metaphor is the runner. Paul wants to run this Christian race and end in joyful victory (V.24). The third metaphor is a steward. As a steward, Paul receives the ministry from the Lord and manages it (V.24). Fourth, Paul sees himself as a herald who preaches the kingdom of God (V.25). Finally, Paul sees himself as a watchman who warns people.

There are three powerful precautions to our movements:

1. **Do not Move out of God's Place.** Our movement should not be due to our peace or pleasures, but according to our placement by God. Paul does not allow trials to move him and he does not move just for tranquility. He says, "None of these things move me." The "things" he is speaking of are those things waiting for him in Jerusalem; beatings, imprisonment, trials, etc.

2. **Do not move out of God's Providence.** Paul wants to finish the course with joy (V.24). In Hebrews 12, Paul speaks of a race. The race is where God has placed us and wants us to be. God does not deal with us through our feelings, but through faith.

3. **Do not Move from God's Purposes.** Paul has received a ministry of the Gospel and grace. Our message is Christ crucified. Even though we support social equality, God has called us to preach the Gospel of Christ. There are three exhortations for movement: 1,be still. 2, be steadfast (1Cor. 15:58). 3, be strong.

There is power in being still and in being in the place where God wants us. Therefore, let's not move ourselves into a mishap.

Transformed by a Transfusion

A blood transfusion can be thought of as a process by which, the blood (life) of one person is taken out of one body and placed into another. This transfer takes place through the blood stream. The Bible says that the life of the body is in the blood.

Biblical salvation is essentially man receiving a transfusion of the righteousness of Jesus Christ. This transfusion is a transaction. Jesus placed His righteousness on us and our unrighteousness on Himself. When the transaction takes place, there is transference and a transformation.

The Lord Jesus is the transformer. He changes our mind, our direction, and our desires. Once God saves us, He wants to change us into the image of Christ. He wants to transfer His Spirit, His life, His light, and His liberation into you. Then, He prepares us for a walk that is worthy of His Name. There are at least three aspects of Christ's Power:

1. **His Life** (John 10:10): Whenever there is transfusion of righteousness, there is an automatic challenge for us to depart from the dominion of darkness. Jesus came to give us life through transformation. If we say we are saved, and there is no restructuring of our minds and our lives, then we are not saved. Salvation is not based on our works, but on our trust and faith in His work. *Salvation is free to us, but it cost Jesus everything.* Jesus brings life, and without Him, there is nothing.

2. **His Light** (John 1:4): The Lord Jesus Christ gives us the ability to see. We will be able to see and discern the things of God (1 Cor. 2:14). Believers are light bearers. Knowing the truth of Jesus provides both outward and inward light. The only reason we have Light is because of His Light. The reason we can see is because of His salvation. The reason we feel the effects and the pain of sin is because we have been indwelt with the Holy Spirit. Transfusion leads to transformation.

3. **His Liberation** (Matt.11:28-29): Church does not make us free; it is only the truth that will make us free. The Word gives us a reason to live. There is no Biblical liberation without learning. We are liberated as we learn truth; then our minds will become renewed and our desires will change. Everyone was liberated when they met Jesus. The woman with the issue of blood had faith, but she needed works to demonstrate her faith. Faith without works

is dead. She had the power, now she needed the participation. The paralyzed man was liberated because they put him in the presence of Jesus Christ.

We are liberated as we learn, lean, and let go. The church has embodied truth, but very few have enabling truth. God is producing a program to make us more like Jesus, and give us the victory, even in the midst of our weakness.

What is Your Temperature?

The tragedy for those who end up in Hell is that they will be fully conscious of the fact that they refused the invitation to salvation. The final Church addressed in the Book of the Revelation, is the Church at Laodecia. It was a church characterized by apostasy. They had formalism, but no fellowship; profession without confession; pretense but no power.

The apostate church is a church that has fallen away from the truth. Even as we examine our own lives, we must be careful that we have not begun to fall away from the truth. God is not in much of what we do. During the indictment of the apostate church, Jesus provides a description of himself, identifies the defect, outlines the deception, confronts the dilemma, and provides the means of deliverance. Jesus refers to himself as The Amen, the Faithful and True Witness, and the Beginning of creation (Rev. 3:14). His description of Himself sets Him apart as the final Word and authority on everything. Not only is He the final Word and Authority, but He is also the Creator of all things. Truly it is in Him that we move, live and have our being. As the Faithful and True Witness, He is the original and expressed image of God.

The defect for which the Church of Laodecia was indicted, was for being neither hot nor cold (Rev. 3:15). *They were playing the role of church but they lacked redemption.* The Lord's response to their defect was to spue them out of His mouth (Rev. 3:16). In spite of the blatant defect within the Church at Laodecia, they thought they were all right. They were deceived about their own condition. The Lord describes them as wretched, miserable, poor, blind, and naked (Rev. 3:17). The Laodecians made room for anything and everything. We all need to examine our spiritual temperature. As always, Jesus has the answer to every one of our dilemmas, as well as the dilemmas of the Church at Laodecia.

The church was in need of salvation to get them out of their spiritually impoverished state. They needed to be clothed in the white raiment, which represents the righteousness of the Lord Jesus Christ. Spiritual nakedness can only be addressed by the righteousness of the Righteous One. Finally, they needed their eyes anointed with eye salve, which is symbolic of the Holy Spirit. Spiritual enlightenment to cure spiritual blindness comes from the Holy Spirit.

Deliverance for the Church at Laodecia rested in the Lord Jesus Christ if they were willing to repent. Jesus says, "Behold I stand at the door and knock; if any man hear my voice, and open up the door, I will come into him and will sup with him, and he with me" (Rev. 3:20).

Jesus is knocking at the door of our hearts in specific areas. His desire is to be the authority over every area of our lives. We forfeit the sweetness of His fellowship when we refuse to respond to His voice.

Where Did You Miss Your Turn?

One of the most disheartening experiences that can happen during a trip, is to find you have been traveling in the wrong direction. You think you are getting closer to your destination, only to discover you are further away from it. We can experience this same disappointment during our spiritual journey. We think we are progressing when we actually are regressing. We assume we are moving forward, only to find ourselves taking steps backward. We are heaven bound but not happy, saved yet sidetracked. It is not uncommon for believers to be misled and end up going in the wrong direction. There are some spiritual barometers that indicate whether we are on the right road. When we are moving in God's will we can expect to experience four things; direction, doctrinal development, a dependent spirit upon God, and deliverance. The opposite is true when we are sidetracked. We lack direction, development, dependence, and deliverance.

Paul, in the Book of Galatians, is trying to convince this group of believers that they are misdirected. Paul begins, in the forth chapter, to use the historical argument to show them they have made a wrong turn. They were religious, but neglecting the relationship. Paul's historical argument begins with a description of what we were, what God did, and who we are now. Paul wants us to understand that we were translated, we are being transformed, and we need to learn to transfer.

1. **What We Were:** Translated (Gal. 4:3-4). We were bound, but when the fullness of time was, God sent forth His Son. We, who were in bondage, have been translated from death and darkness, into life and light. We were children, in bondage, and were servants, but now we have been set free, and placed into the family of God as sons and daughters. We enter the family through regeneration (being born again), but we enjoy the privileges of the family through adoption. Our adoption allows us to receive immediately, all the privileges granted to an adult child who has come of age. We don't have to wait, but we must learn to appropriate our status. Many of the frustrations in our walk are the result of our inability to appropriate who we are. We must grow so that we are able to experience the abundant life that Christ has already given us. "I've come that they may have life and life more abundantly." When we have been translated, God sets up a direction; He begins to develop us, He teaches us to be dependent, and He delivers us.

2. **What God Did:** Transformed (Gal. 4:6-7). *Transformation means God has a divine plan to conform us into the image of His Son.* We must be taught what to choose and what to refuse. Our development enables us to make right choices, to overcome our fears, and to depend upon the God of our salvation. "Whom he did foreknow, him he did predestinate to be conformed to the image of His Son" (Rom. 8:29). Paul asked them why they would return to a prison when they had been liberated? Likewise, why would we return to law when grace has set us free? Why return to religion when we have a relationship?

3. **What We Are:** Transferring (Heb. 4:16) Because we have been translated and are being transformed, we must learn to transfer. Translation provides our position and allows us to enjoy privilege. Transformation develops us so that we can appropriate God's power. Transferring allows us to experience God's peace. We must stop trying and start trusting. Stop working and start waiting. Stop pouting and start praying.

Have you made a wrong turn? Get back on track, let go, and let God.

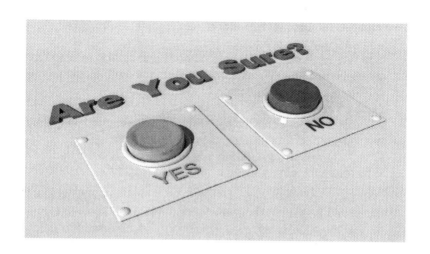

SPIRITUAL WARFARE

Submit yourselves therefore to God.

Resist the devil, and he will flee from you.

James 4:7

Blocked By My Baggage

One of the most mentally crippling circumstances one may find him or herself in, is to be confined in chains within a psychiatric cell. In a spiritual sense, a sin can short circuit our shouts, jolt our joy, and postpone our provisions. This is the sin of an unforgiving spirit. When we have been hurt, we are not always able to let the perpetrator free. If we continue to hold him or her captive in anger, we cause ourselves irreparable damage. We must release those who have hurt us. We have no right to hold them hostage.

The three facets of an unforgiving spirit are the bondages, the barometers, and the breakthroughs. In Matthew 5:23-24, Jesus says if there is anyone who has anything against us, do not come to the altar. In other words, we are not to come praising God when we have an issue with someone or someone has an issue with us.

1. **An Unforgiving Spirit Binds us and Blocks our Liberty**. When we do not forgive, we create an internal strife that chokes communion and communication. An unforgiving spirit holds another person responsible for the pain in our life. Do not hold people hostage, because God is not holding you hostage.

2. **An Unforgiving Spirit is a Barometer of Inner Spiritual Baggage**. When we cannot forgive someone, we have major spiritual problems. The Greek word for *forgiveness* means to release or to cancel a debt. Jesus prayed, "Forgive us our trespasses as we forgive those who have trespassed against us." No one in the church is perfect. Thus, we must forgive. In Matthew 18, we learn about principles on discipline in the church. If someone is in open sin and it can be verified by two or three witnesses, one person is to go to the offender and plead with him to repent of the sin. If the offender does not respond, take two or three more to beg him to repent (V.16). If he still does not respond, tell it to the church. The church must also beg him to repent. Then, if he does not respond, excommunicate him (V.17). When the church takes on these principles, then, "what is bound on earth is already bound in heaven and what is loosed on earth is already loosed in heaven" (V.18). Furthermore, where two or three witnesses are in Christ's name, He is in the midst (V.20). This promise is in the context of church discipline.

Peter asks Jesus how often he should forgive another (V.21). Jesus says seventy times seven, that is, unlimited times (V.22). To explain this truth, Jesus teaches a parable (vv.23-35). A slave owed a king an unimaginable amount of money. He was, therefore, to be sold for payment. The slave pleaded with the king for patience. The king had compassion and forgave the debt. But, that servant found another servant who owed him a much smaller amount and demanded repayment. This debtor also pleaded for patience, but was instead cast into prison. When the king heard, he threw the unforgiving servant into prison. This is the pattern of the Father (v. 35). When we do not forgive others, God does not forgive us. We have no right to hold people hostage by remaining angry with them.

3. **An Unforgiving Spirit can have a Breakthrough.**

There were three people who were hurt by others but, through the grace of God, they managed to do the right thing. In Job 42:10, God said He would restore everything Job lost after he reconciled with the three friends who condemned him. Joseph, in Genesis 50:15-19, forgives the brothers who sold him into slavery. Jesus asks the Father to forgive the people.

Forgiveness is a release that brings rest. We must say, "I forgive you." Jesus commands that we release the other person, and then the truth will make us free!

The Battle Behind the Scenes

The greatest battle of Spiritual warfare is that of the elect angels against the evil and fallen ones. This battle is behind the scenes as Satan attempts to interfere, influence, and inflict pain upon God's people. Satan is organized and tries to duplicate God.

According to Ezekiel 28, Lucifer was the anointed cherub who was covered with precious stones. He was bright, brilliant, and God had built in him many kinds of music. He is called the prince of the power of the air. He controls the economical, political, and religious systems. He is only allowed to rule this world temporarily.

Satan wants to block our comprehension of the Word so that we cannot hear from God and experience His comfort. He wants to interfere with our peace, praise, and power. His job is to confuse us. In Daniel chapter 10, we come face to face with a cosmic warfare. It is in this warfare that we see five critical encounters:

1. **The Dimensions of Daniel's Anguish** (Dan. 10:1-4). Daniel was troubled. He had been praying and fasting, because only a few Jews were returning to Jerusalem. Once they were taken out of the land, they became comfortable with Babylon and they lost their desire to return. Daniel saw that those who were going back had heartaches and he understood the suffering that the Jews had to go through in the future.

2. **The Description of the Angel** (Dan. 10:5-9) - The angel was bright and had a glorious appearance, because it was carrying the rays of God's Shekinah Glory. If we spent time in God's presence we too, would light up. Angels have the power under the authority of God; to come down to earth either as male or female. The Bible tells us, "Be not forgetful to entertain strangers: for thereby some have entertained angels unawares" (Heb. 13:2).

3. **The Declaration of the Angel** (Dan. 10:10-17). Daniel had been praying for three weeks for an understanding of God's will, but there was a hindrance. There was a cosmic war with Michael the archangel, Gabriel, the angels, and Satan. There will be many hindrances throughout our lifetimes; marriages, families, and minds. These battles are satanic. There is only one Name that makes demons tremble and when you call on that Name, "Jesus," there is power.

4. **The Duty of the Angel** (Dan. 10:18-19). Gabriel strengthens and encourages Daniel. We all need encouragement on our job, in our marriage, and in the church. When you feel like giving up, God will send a Word.

5. **The Determination of the Angel** (Dan. 10:20-21). The angel went back to fight Satan. There is warfare behind the scenes. Light is fighting darkness. Filth is fighting purity. Trust is fighting un-trust. "We are not fighting against flesh and blood but against principalities, powers, dominions, and thrones." Therefore, *pray in the spirit and put on the whole armor of God.*

Being Free

Love, Truth, and Freedom are three of the most misused and misunderstood words of the English vocabulary. Love is confused with legalism, license, and lust. Truth is misinterpreted by trial and error, and freedom is misunderstood as free-will. All of us need to be freed from something: histories, hurts, and habits. Biblical freedom is predicated upon a Biblical faith.

John chapter 8 is about contrasts. In verse 11, there is the contrast between grace and law; verses 12-20 contrasts light and darkness, verses 21-30 contrasts life and death, while verses 31- 40 contrasts bondage and freedom. Jesus gives us a formula for freedom: there is no spiritual freedom unless we are born again. "If you continue in my Word, then are ye my disciples indeed: and you shall know the truth, and the truth shall make you free" (John 8: 32). There are four aspects of freedom that come from being born again:

1. **We are Free from Satan's Destruction**. Satan's objective is to stop salvation by blinding the "eyes" (minds) of people. Satan is trying to stunt the believer's growth by sowing seeds of discord. Staying in the Word allows us to hear God's voice. James 3:17 says that God's wisdom is pure, peaceable, easy to be entreated, and full of mercy.

2. **We are Free from Satan's Deceptions**. II Thessalonians 2:3-12 illustrates how Satan approaches us with a design to deceive. When we disobey continuously, we lose our light, our love, our joy, our peace, our fellowship, our confidence and possibly our health. The Holy Spirit is restraining sin and stopping Satan from having free reign in our lives, and God gives us discernment to make right decisions, as we continue in the Word.

3. **We are Free from Satan's Dominions**. John 16:7 says that we will not lose, because we have a Paraclete: the Holy Spirit, our Comforter. John 17:1-3 tells us that we will not lose our Pardon, because our salvation is secure. We have Perseverance, thus, we cannot be lost V.12. We will never lose our Place, because we have a guarantee that we will see Jesus.

4. **We are Free from Satan's Devices**. "For the weapons of our warfare are not carnal, but mighty through God to the pulling down of strong holds" (II Cor. 10:4). The word *stronghold* means fortress, something that Satan keeps using against us. If we continue in the Word, the Truth will make us free and the Holy Spirit will perform surgery to tear down the strongholds in our lives.

Charge Your Battery

Each person who is enlisted into military service is sworn to the commitment to defend his country. This commitment requires that personal agendas and all personal rights be set aside. The soldier must submit to and defend his country. There is a spiritual parallel. Each Believer is sworn into God's army. The serious disciple (follower of Jesus Christ), must set aside his or her own personal rights and submit to the authority of the Lord Jesus Christ.

In I Tim. 3:10, Paul challenged Timothy to teach sound doctrine, and in verses II -17, Paul exhorted Timothy to remain committed to the Gospel of Jesus Christ. Paul closes the first chapter with a charge to defend the faith. He gives a soldier marching orders. Timothy's orders contain three main instructions: fight, keep the faith, and endure the friction.

1. **Instructions to Fight** (1 Tim. 1:18): Paul reminds Timothy that when he was called, there were prophecies associated with his life (V.16). When God calls us, He has a plan and purpose for our lives. Our lives no longer belong to us, but we have a divine purpose to glorify Him and build His kingdom. Because God has a plan to develop and deploy us, Satan also has a plan to destroy us. We must understand that, "we are not wrestling against flesh and blood, but against principalities," and that "The weapons of our warfare are not carnal but mighty through God" (I Cor 10:4). *Satan engages us in warfare on two major fronts.* He has strategies he employs, which work on us from the outside in; and we have strongholds, which he taps into, that work from the inside out. His strategic battles are the arguments he presents against the knowledge of God. If we are not grounded in the Word of God (our weapon), Satan will dislodge us. Strongholds, on the other hand, are our own fleshly thinking patterns that Satan can tap into, at will, to get us to react to life out of the flesh, instead of through the Spirit. We must learn to battle in our mind. Bring every thought captive (2 Cor. 10:5). We can't rely on our strength; we are instructed in Eph. 6 to be strong in the Lord. It is His battle.

2. **Instructions to Keep the Faith** (1 Tim. 1:19): What we believe affects our behavior. Faith operates like our clock, and our conscience is our alarm that rings when we are about to stray. We cut off our conscience just like we cut off our alarm clocks. We must fight to maintain integrity, morality, and purity.

3. **Instructions to Endure Friction** (1 Tim. 1:19-20): The final charge was for Timothy to endure friction. In this walk, conflict and confrontation are inevitable because Satan is as a roaring lion, seeking whom he may devour. We will experience external friction (vv.19, 20) and confrontation, as well as internal friction. The battleground for the internal friction involves three areas: the mind, the heart, and the mouth. The Bible tells us that as a man thinketh in his heart, so is he, therefore, we must keep our hearts with all diligence. We must endure the friction with confidence that we are already victorious.

We are charged to fight the good warfare, keep the faith, and endure the friction. The Believer's walk is not an easy one, but it is a victorious one!

Confused by His Covering

Combat soldiers fully understand the importance of wearing camouflaged fatigues. The fatigues present a three-fold problem to the enemy. The enemy blends into the surroundings un-noticed. He comes as a wolf in sheep's clothing to disguise his motives and methods. He blinds onlookers and masquerades behind personal perceptions and purposes. He baffles the people of God, as he moves through ministry, actually using truth to confound the defenders of truth.

In Biblical warfare, a child of God must be prayed up to discern the full arsenal of the enemy. Satan does not wear a red suit and carry a pitchfork. He is too wise. He can look, act, sing, preach, and walk like Christians. It takes a mature Believer, who is called a father in the faith, to discern his tactics. In the context of 2 Cor. 2, Paul will expose three of the devil's tactics, as he tricks the saved and unsaved.

1. **Blended by Satan**: Satan's workers are always disguised. We are in an era of a false gospel, a false spirit, and a false-Christ. Satan is hiding in evil and error. Judas blended in, but he was satanic in his demeanor. He had a personal agenda. There are people in our lives who can blend in and give us the impression that they are for us, but are really against us. Many preachers are swaying people with their concepts and philosophies that are not biblically based, and the sheep are eating poison.

2. **Blinded by Satan**: Whatever is in our minds is from either God or Satan. Satan blinds us in our leading and in our liberation. He wants us to make decisions based on our feelings and not through faith. He blinds the leading of the Holy Spirit and wants to promote our personal dreams and visions. Satan loves to trick us. He will study us and give us exactly what we want, but will never show us the full consequences of taking it.

3. **Baffled by Satan**: Satan wants to move us out from where God has placed us. He wants to move us out of our homes, from our relationships, and out of ministry. Satan wants us to give up our faith, hope, and peace. He wants to try to stop us from doing what we are doing for God. We need to wake up and know that God is able to work out our deliverance.

When we are a true disciple of Jesus, there is a fearfulness for the work of the Lord. We are fruitful in our work and a facilitator of sound doctrine. While, Satan wants us to be comfortable in deception and sin. Whatever Satan brings to us, God will bring us out of, if we are His children. Thanks be to God who gives us the victory in Christ Jesus!

Marching to the Drum Beat:

Marching orders are given prior to any military mission. These orders remind the soldier of the purpose, the provisions, and the plans for the battle. In the concluding chapter of I Timothy, Paul urges Timothy to be on guard for false teachers. False teaching not only involves doctrinal error but also involves the motives and the makeup of the teacher. God is constantly scrutinizing everything and everyone. Paul described the make-up, motives, and mishaps of false teachers earlier in the chapter. He now addresses Timothy as the man of God, indicating that he is one who teaches and preaches the Word of God. The man of God rebukes, reproves, and instructs others in righteousness. How do we recognize a man or woman of God? There are three indicators of a man of God laid out in 1 Timothy.

1. **What the Man of God Flees** (1 Tim. 1:11). The man of God must flee certain things. He must be like a fugitive who flees with the intent of never being caught. Running is not the action of a coward, but rather, a show of strength. In Genesis, Joseph ran from Potiphar's wife. David ran from Saul. The Godly man must flee or separate himself from the practices, philosophy, and pollution of sin. We must flee form sexual immorality, youthful lusts, and idolatry. Sin has a philosophy from which we must flee. Things may look good and be appealing to our logic and rationale, but it is of the flesh and not of God. We must separate ourselves from the philosophy of sin, run from the pollution of sin, and watch our associations because bad company corrupts good morals.

2. **What the Man of God Follows** (1 Tim. 1:11). A Godly man pursues righteousness, which is a matter of personal integrity. Righteousness deals with those things that are done when no one is looking. They follow after godliness, pursuing practical piety. Godliness does not have to do so much with the outward actions but rather, the inner attitude. A man or woman of God must pursue faith. Faith involves confident trust in the Lord Jesus Christ, as well as following Truth. Those who follow after, and pursue as a lifestyle, unconditional love and meekness, will be recognized as those who march after the drumbeat of the Holy Spirit. Because of their faith and the abiding presence of the Holy Spirit, the godly will live each day in expectation, waiting for God to do something.

3. **What the Man Fights** (1 Tim. 1:12). We must dress in the whole armor of God. We must wear our helmet of salvation, breastplate of righteousness, and shield of faith which covers everything. We must have our feet shod with the preparation of the gospel, and carry the sword of the Spirit, which is the Word of God. The man of God must remember he is in a battle. The good news is that he is not fighting for victory he is fighting from victory. Greater is He that is in us than he that is in the world. Furthermore, we must remain faithful. "I give thee charge . . . thou keep this commandment without spot, un-rebukeable, until the appearing of our Lord Jesus Christ" (V.13).

Whose drumbeat are you marching to? Would anyone recognize you as a man or woman of God? Are you fleeing, following, fighting, and remaining faithful?

Sign of the Times:

Previews in a movie theater, are known as coming attractions. They are a select group of short clips from films that actually have a much larger plot than depicted. Spiritually, the Word of God serves as a preview of what is coming. Prophetically, God gives us specific scriptures to let us know what will come to pass. Promotionally, we know what is coming to pass: Jesus is going to be recognized as Lord of all. One of the laws of hermeneutics, interpreting the Word, is that everything in the New Testament is hidden in the Old Testament, and everything in the Old  Testament is open in the New Testament. In 1 John 2:18, God gives us a preview of Satan's strategies. John tells us of Satan's person and his poison. The person is not here yet, but the poison is already in place. His plan is four-fold:

1. **Satan's Strategy**. We are being deceived with deceptive devices that are undetectable. The deception is, Satan partially blinds us to the will of God. He does this through our hurts and disappointments. When we are hurt and disappointed, he is able to weave his way in rendering us open to his attacks. We have to be open to the Word of God constantly. His deceptive ways started in Genesis 3:15. God cursed the physical and the spiritual serpent saying, "and I will put enmity between thee and the woman, and between thy seed and her seed; it shall bruise thy head, and thou shalt bruise his heel." The woman's seed is Jesus Christ and all believers. The serpent's seed is the anti-Christ and all unbelievers. His seed is only going to bruise Jesus through suffering and death, but Jesus is coming back! The woman's seed, Jesus and all Believers, will crush Satan's head. Romans 16:20 says, "and the God of peace shall bruise Satan under your feet shortly." God is going to use believers to crush Satan right now, and render him inoperative as we yield to the Holy Spirit.

2. **Satan's Seductions**. Satan not only deceives, he divides. His objective is in the spirit of the anti-Christ that brings division into the house of God. He can use our mouths and opinions to divide. One of the things God hates is the sowing of discord among the brethren. Rom. 16:17, "Now I beseech you, brethren, mark them which cause divisions and offences contrary to the doctrine which ye have learned; and avoid them." Point

them out, and if they keep it up, put them out. This is a Biblical reason for excommunication.

3. **Satan's Sinister**. Satan destroys by planting seeds years before he makes his move. He specializes in playing with our minds using his destructive strategies and doctrinal seductions.

4. **Satan's Silencing**. Jesus will wipe out the anti-Christ. We have already won the war; God has already crushed Satan under our feet. The anti-Christ can't hurt us. Satan can't harm us. Evil can't get us because greater is He that's in us, than he that's in the world. God is going to heal, comfort, soothe, and strengthen us, because we are a new creation. It was at Calvary that we received the victory; We are the elect of God! No weapon formed against us will prosper.

THE PROFIT
OF
OUR PAIN

Wherein ye greatly rejoice, though now for

a season, if need be, ye are in heaviness

through manifold temptations:

1 Peter 1:6

Fire Testing:

Being Tested in the Fire

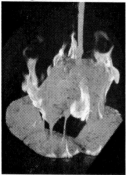

God chooses to challenge His children with a curriculum designed to change their character, their confidence, and their confusion. A believer is centered in three different modes of faith. Once we are born again (elected of God) we are placed into One Lord, One Faith, and One Baptism. Faith is an ability to transfer our troubles to God; it is an abiding of trust that leads to tranquility. This is done moment by moment.

Three things happen in the testing mode, which produces faith. God begins with:

1. **The Process of Pain** (Character): Pain can change our character. We need our character changed because, in Hebrews 10:26, we see that God is a God of Holiness. He has a day of reckoning that will punish sinners. The Spirit of God carves our character through pain. Pain is a process that leads to a product: patience. James tells us that the fire testing of our faith works patience. In the Greek, the word *perseverance* means the ability to stick it out when things get rough. God teaches us His love as we are confronted with trouble. Job lost all that he had; he was infected with an incurable disease, and his friends turned their backs on him. Then, he had a change in his perception of himself and God. Job said, "I have heard of thee by the hearing of the ear: but now mine eye seeth thee" (Job. 42:5). Therefore, God places us in pain to work out our character.

2. **The Product of Power** (Confidence): God will deliver us continuously as we place confidence in Him (Heb. 10:35). *Faith is seeing evidence without being an eyewitness.* Faith says, "Lord, I can believe you without seeing anything." We must believe that He is going to fix the problems in our lives, marriages, and families. Like the Old Testament elders , we obtain a good report, by the confidence we place in God (Heb. 11:2).

3. **The Place of Providence** (Confusion): Trusting in God's providence helps erase our confusion. God's sovereignty placed us by His providence on salvation's track. We may still have some encumbrances in our lives. God wants to deal with our confusion in the midst of our conflict. Even the Lord's chastening is for our good. Faith in God's providential sovereignty produces triumph instead of trouble.

This walk is not about our feelings, but about our faith. We have the victory because Jesus lives. Without Him, we can do nothing.

God's Correction After We Crash

Joshua - Chapter 8

A great deal of our conflict is directly connected to our compromising God's counsel. Our evil prevents our enablement and our power is preempted by our fleshly plans and lack of purity. Thus, we wait, and yet, we are wounded; we cry, but we are still crippled. If we are in a place of grief, this message is for us. What happens when we fail God and are defeated in our lives? When we begin to listen to God there is a venue for victory, a proposal for power, and a remedy for rest.

However, many of us are prideful and refuse to admit that we have fallen or failed. Some of us have been devastated and still will not admit it. Depression and frustration can make us physically and mentally ill. It is time to stop being religious and get real. We should all remember that there are dry times in our spiritual lives. Joshua was in a place of drought, because Achan's sin caused Israel to be defeated. Joshua felt like giving up and he even blamed God for what happened to Israel. Therefore, Joshua needed to hear God's counsel, correction and convocation.

1. **God's Counsel after the Crash**. Many times we must be still and do nothing (Psalm 46:10). God will give inspiration and instruction. God tells Joshua to fear not because fear had stripped Joshua of his confidence. When we feel defeated, fear has overcome. Satan uses fear to keep us in bondage. We feel fear for our children, relationships, career, etc. Fear is the opposite of faith and "without faith it is impossible to please God" (Heb. 11:6). We need confidence to pray right and to overcome the state of being dismayed. Fear not, faint not, and do not worry about the future. God is with us.

2. **God's Correction after the Crash**. God is calling for committed and faithful people to help the body of Christ. When we are chosen for service, we will be given orders. It is not our job to question, but it is our job to submit to leadership. If we are going to conquer after we crash, we must make corrections in our lives. We must not allow weaknesses to keep us in bondage. Through the power of the Holy Spirit, let's clean up our thinking, talking, and walking.

3. **God's Convocation after the Crash**. When we make up our minds to worship God in Spirit and in truth, it will cost us. When we come to God, we should have knowledge of God in

our heads, compassion in our hearts, and an offering in our hands, to bring glory to God. The first day of the week, Sunday, is for worship. God requires that we come to church (1 Cor. 16:2). Church helps us to receive the gifts that minister to the body. Worship will heal our wounds.

Let God counsel, correct, and call you unto Himself after a crash.

Grace That Grants Us Favor

II Corinthians 8 & 9

One of the greatest privileges afforded God's people is an appreciation for a dedication to the grace of God. God's grace is receiving love when we don't deserve it. It's an opportunity for the outcast, favor towards the fragmented, and a pardon in place of our pollution. Until we grow in grace, we will not really be blessed. Too often people will accept a certain portion of the Word but reject another portion. This will stunt their growth. They are deceived and not in the center of God's will. Paul the Apostle, begins to suggest grace giving to the church of Corinth: a giving that involves surrender, submission, and sharing, all to the Glory of God. Our giving is just as spiritual as our prayer lives and our walk with the Lord.

1. **Grace-Giving is Giving Beyond our Abilities** (2 Cor. 8:1-4). The Corinthians gave beyond what they had, with a joyful attitude. We also, should be supporting the work, the will, and the Word of God. When we give of ourselves sacrificially, then God will give us a mind to work for Him. God does not want our money; He wants us. However, when we do not tithe, we struggle. When our fists are closed, God cannot put anything in them. Truly, God loves a cheerful giver.

2. **Grace-Giving is Giving with a Willing Attitude** (2 Cor. 8:5-7). We can trouble our own houses by mismanaging our money. Many of us do not have a problem rejoicing when we hear messages about suffering and how Jesus will bring us through. But we must also rejoice when we are being instructed to give.

3. **Grace-Giving is Giving with an Understanding of Spiritual Association** (2 Cor.8: 8-9). We are rich in Christ through eternal life. Jesus came to save sinners. He got up from His throne, became a man, went to the cross, and died to get us out of hell. He who was rich, became poor. Why shouldn't we give a portion of our earnings for the work of Christ when Jesus gave His all? Everything we have belongs to Jesus.

4. **Grace-Giving is giving in Appreciation** (2 Cor. 8:10-15). God wants us to manage what He gives us according to His Word. When we support the work of the church, souls are saved, lives become changed, and workers can perform what God is calling them to do. When we are committed to the work of the

Lord, He will guide our steps, grant us favor, and guarantee our blessings. There is a need, not only for us to give our money, but also our time and talents.

As we sow bountifully, we will reap bountifully. Giving is not about money coming back into your hands, sometimes it is about God opening up doors of opportunities. God shall supply all of our needs according to His riches in Glory. When we invest in Jesus, God is able to give us increase through taking care of our children, putting bread on our tables, and clothes on our bodies.

Although He was rich, He became poor that we might be rich. Thank you Jesus for sacrificing Yourself! Thank you Jesus for Your giving.

How God Moves Us:

Peter was a leading disciple of Jesus Christ. He was called the stone that was built on a Rock, called Jesus. He fell, was frustrated, lost his sense of faith, and yet God used him mightily. Jesus told him, "Simon, Simon, Satan has desired to sift you as wheat, but I have prayed for you that your faith fail not, and when you are converted feed my lambs." The book of Peter is about grace; love we do not deserve. In grace, there cannot be a penalty, there is no payment, and there is no punishment when we fall short.

Mercy is not receiving what we deserve. The enemy cannot have our souls, but he will certainly come after us. His job is to stop our testimonies about Jesus, and to prevent us from being encouraged in the faith. Peter warns us to be alert, be careful, and be vigilant, because the devil is seeking whom he may devour (1 Pet. 5:8). Although we may go through difficult circumstances, Satan wants to divert all of us from the things of God. Grace and Mercy illuminate three aspects of the Christian life:

1. **The Savior**: Our Savior is a Savior of grace. There is nothing that we can do to earn grace. Grace keeps us, repairs us, and resuscitates us. *When we want to give up, grace will show up.* Our strength comes from God and Him alone. God does not want us to trust in anything, but Him, because our weaknesses are perfected in Him.

2. **The Suffering**: God said to be encouraged no matter what trials and troubles are in our lives. The trials and trouble are needed. Nothing is going to come into our lives unless God allows it. There is a benefit in suffering; He is not trying to punish us, but help us. We must start to see our suffering from the perspective of God. I Thes. 5:18 says, "In everything give thanks, for this is the will of God in Christ Jesus concerning you." We must learn to praise God through our suffering. Knowing that while we suffer, God is maturing us. He will build character through suffering. Every time God put character in one of His children, it was always on the heel of a catastrophe. Until we go through suffering, we cannot develop. He will equip us through suffering. God will allow us to suffer, in order to bring obedience into our lives. Once God takes us through, we will be able to stand!

3. **The Steadfastness**: When we are mature in Him, we will be able to stand still and know that He is God, even when a storm is raging. He wants to establish and strengthen us, so that whatever comes our way, we will be able to handle it. Our suffering will make us more like Jesus.

No matter what, He wants us to praise Him. Thanking Him for the troubles, trials, and tribulations will enable us to shout, "Now unto Him who is able to keep *ME* from falling . . ."

The Profit of our Pain

II Corinthians 12:7-9

What do we do when God says no! Throughout scripture there is a principle of privilege; that where much is given much more is required. The greater the light of revelation is in our lives, the greater the load of responsibility. Leadership positions should not be taken lightly when we serve the Lord in certain capacities. Every time we step up, God's requirements go up.

A position affects our privilege and this may bring us pain. Every Believer should have a theology on pain. When pain comes, we need to know how to deal with it. Our pain could be an instrument of God's displeasure. If we are foolish, we will ultimately reap the foolishness that we have sown. Pain may be an indicator of God's direction. It could also be an instruction to depend on Him. Jesus wants us to stop trying to work it out, wait on Him, and trust in Him.

When we are under His wings, He speaks loudly in our pain and lovingly when we are at peace. God's intent is not to hurt us, but to help us. God does not always see our plights as we see them, He sees His purpose. He is more concerned about His glory and our good, than He is about the temporary grief that we go through. In 2 Cor. 12, Paul will give us some perspective on his pain.

1. **The Privilege of God's Vision** (2 Cor. 12:1-6). God's glory is greater than our good. When someone close to us dies, we are hurt because God took someone from us; however, as the eulogy is preached souls hear the Word and get saved. If He had not taken them, the others may have gone to hell. Many times we pray for God to bring our children back to church, but God may have to take them through something to get them to come back. We cannot ask God to do something and then instruct Him how to do it. God gave Paul a plan for this age, a preview of paradise, and a perspective of things that he did not understand; things that he was not allowed to talk about. It was this privilege that led to his pain.

2. **The Pain of God's Healing** (2 Cor. 12:7-8). God knows what is best for us. Our pain may be a preventive tool from sinning. Our prayers will not alter God's purpose. Paul prayed three times, and God still said, "No". When suffering comes into our lives it can either make us bitter or better. When we accept the pain, God will do something constructive with it, and give us a peace

that surpasses all understanding. Peace comes when we agree with God. God knows what is best in every situation. He is all-wise.

3. **The Praise of God's Victory** (2 Cor. 12:9-10). Grace is sufficient for everything that we need. Whatever we need, God can provide. When we become weak, He gives us His strength. God wants us to get low, so He can bring us up higher.

God has a purpose, plan, and perspective for our pain, that will end with our profit.

MAKING THE RIGHT DECISIONS

If any of you lack wisdom, let him ask
of God, that giveth to all men liberally,
and upbraideth not;
and it shall be given him.

James 1:5

Brotherly Love

The characteristic that distinguishes a Christian from a non-believer, is their ability to demonstrate brotherly love. Just like a wounded bird cannot fly, a wounded Christian cannot demonstrate Biblical love. Whenever we see a Believer who is struggling with loving others, we know that person is wounded and in need of healing. Love of the brethren is the glue that holds the fellowship together. It is this brotherly love, found in the Book of Acts, that enabled them to come together and hold everything in common. In fact, the exhortation in Ephesians is to endeavor to keep the peace. We must painstakingly keep the peace and unity of the brethren. Jesus told his disciples, *"they will know you are my disciples by the way you love one another."* Jesus, also, gave us a new commandment, *"love one another."* As the writer of Hebrews concludes the book, he continues his transition from doctrine to duty, and from profession to practice. The writer exhorts us to live out what Christ commands. In the thirteenth chapter, we are encouraged to live out our faith in three areas:

1. **Live Out our Faith by Sustaining Brotherly Love**. We are to let brotherly love continue (Heb. 13:1). Our need to have sustaining love deals with our Christian hospitality. The encouragement is not only for how we treat other Believers, but also strangers because some have entertained angels unaware (V.2). Abraham, in the eighteenth chapter of Genesis, was hospitable to strangers who turned out to be angels. As we love, we should remember those who are struggling and are being persecuted, as if we also were in bondage. It is always easier to show forth compassion if we put ourselves in the place of others. As we think of those who are not so easy to love, remember it is the brokenness in them that prevents them from being lovable.

2. **Live Out our Faith by Maintaining Sexual Purity**. In the context of marriage, sexual relationships are pure and holy. Outside of marriage, sex is sin. The writer had to remind his audience that marriage was honorable before the sight of God, because marriage had begun to lose its luster. Forbidding marriage and abstaining from certain foods are signs of the last days (I Tim. 4:1-3). The only context for sexual relationships is marriage; anything else is not God's will.

3. **Live Out our Faith by Being Satisfied**. Our lives as Believers should be marked by contentment. *"Let your conduct be without*

covetousness and be content with such things as you have" (Heb. 13:5). Some of us are never contented. We always want more, or want what others have. In what areas of our lives are we expressing discontentment? We need to work on cultivating a spirit of thanksgiving, for it is the Lord who says He will never leave us nor forsake us. "Godliness with contentment is great gain" (I Tim. 6:6). Begin to thank God for all that He has provided.

Are we sustaining brotherly love? Are we maintaining sexual purity? Does it appear to others that we are satisfied, or are we always complaining? Sustain love, maintain purity, and remain satisfied, through the power of the Holy Spirit.

Called to Cooperate

Anyone chosen or elected by God immediately experiences an irresistible and irrevocable call to God's program. *Irresistible* means we cannot fight it. *Irrevocable* means there is no going back once we have been called. The call gives the Believer direction, discernment, dedication, new desire, and ultimately, deliverance. The call is proof that everything is going to be alright. When God calls us out, we can rest assured that He is in the process of working something out for our good and His Glory. The call trans-lates our problems into purpose, and our delays and difficulties into deliverance.

Paul wrote the book of Romans on his third visit to Corinth, in 58-60 A.D. While in Corinth, Paul had a chance to see the many sins taking place, and he decided to write to the Romans about sin, sanctification and salvation. The first three chapters are about condemnation (all men are guilty, Jew and Gentiles). Chapter 4 defines what justification is; it means to be declared right. Chapters 5-7 explain Positional Sanctification and Practical Sanctification. Positional Sanctification means that the minute we believe in Jesus we are perfect, because God no longer sees us, He sees Jesus. Practical Sanctification is a process of progressive sanctification by which we grow in Grace. Chapter 8 explains Glorification. Chapters 9, 10, and 11 deal with Israel. In Chapter 12, Paul begs us to conform ourselves for worship. In Chapter 13, Paul presents the civil laws of the community. In Chapter 14, he outlines the conscience of the Believers and the differences between weaker and stronger brethren. Chapter 15 is about the Resurrection, chapter 16 the Collection. Chapter 17 includes: the Call; God's plan to perfect His people, God's process, to cause everything to work together for good, and God's power, to bring peace in the midst of any predicament.

Everyone will hear about Jesus, but not all will receive salvation. Ephesians tells us we have been chosen and elected by Him before the foundation of the world. He called us with a heavenly and elective calling. He is going to correct and edify us through a process called sanctification.

1. **The Privilege of the Call** (Rom. 1:1-2): Paul, a prisoner of Jesus Christ, called to be an apostle, was a planner, preacher, and promoter who was sent and separated. We are saints by calling, not saints by good works.

2. **The Passion of the Call** (Rom. 1:8-15). As we are thankful for others, the Holy Spirit gives us the persuasion to say "thank You" in everything. We facilitate prayers for others with passion. We find love for others and we are debtors to others. We are eager to talk about Jesus Christ.

3. **The Power of the Call** (Rom. 1:16-17). The call includes three aspects: (a) Origin, Paul asks, How long will you keep quiet about what you say you believe? (b) Operation, if we start to believe in the person of Jesus Christ, then it will start a work in us. It sends a power that will not only save but sustain. (c) Outcome, we were summoned by election, sanctified by correction, but we will become holy through perfection (maturity).

Conditional Sin

One of the greatest experiments ever performed; one which taught us a great deal about environment and conditioning, was conducted by one of the great behaviorists, Pavlov. While using a stimulus and response technique, he concluded that no one can become conditioned without realizing it. In his experiments, Pavlov used mice to react in a prescribed way, while conditioning them with the use of a bell and a gratifying reward. The bell was the stimulus drawing the mice's attention, and the reward was granted after the appropriate response. Much the same way, all of us have been conditioned by our past, our traditions, and Satan. Satan rings bells to alert us with a false stimulus, and he has a deceptive reward to initiate in us a desired response.

1. **Our Reasoning**: The great Apostle Peter was a conditioned man. His stimulus was; his Jewish heritage, his reward was the approval of his Jewish brothers, his response was separation from Gentiles. However, before we criticize Peter, we must examine ourselves. There are conditions that exist, where we seem to do the very thing we despise, or we seem to do what we said we would not do. What bondage! According to the text, after the important conference described in Acts 15, Peter came from Jerusalem to Antioch. He had enjoyed fellowship with all the Believers (Jews and Gentiles alike).

2. **Our Relapses**: There was a root cause for Peter's relapsing with separating himself, a Jew, from Gentile Believers; the root cause was fear. Fear had always prompted the impulsive Peter to choose a wrong action. Case #1 – Peter walking on the water. Case #2 – Peter rebuking Jesus not to die. Case #3 – Peter on Mt. Transfiguration. Case #4 – Peter cutting off Malcus' ear. Peter, like us, was without excuse; Jesus had taught him valuable lessons (Mt. 15-20). The Holy Spirit re-emphasized those lessons when He sent Peter to the home of Cornelius (Acts 10). You see, Peter's freedom was threatened by Peter's fear. Timothy was fearful, as was, Moses and Jeremiah. However, Peter's fear was different because it caused two tragedies, which led to his fall. His fears made him a hypocrite, which is the meaning of the word *dissembled*. Peter pretended that his actions were motivated by faithfulness, when they were really motivated by fear. Peter even led others astray (through seperating himself from the Gentile Believers).

3. **Our Rebuke**: In Galatians 2:11-14, Paul openly confronts Peter for denying five major doctrines, through drawing away from all Gentile believers, due to the arrival of his Jewish brethren. Likewise, our decisions cause us to deny the very principles that we believe and preach to others. Whenever we are confronted with our sin, our response should be repentence.

4. **Our Restoration**: Peter not only repented, turned away, from his sin, but he did not resent Paul for his rebuke (2 Pet. 3:15-16).

"But the God of all grace, who hath called us unto His eternal glory by Christ Jesus, after that you have suffered awhile, make you perfect, establish, strengthen and settle you."

Family Feud

Family squabbles, sibling rivalry, and foolish contentions, are a part of everyone's family experience. Parents have to act as arbitrators. In the past, although trouble and disagreements were a part of every family, it was a known fact that going outside the family to a neighbor or a stranger to settle the issues, was unacceptable. Family matters were resolved behind closed doors. Paul had to address how disputes in the family of God should be resolved (1 Cor. 6). His strong exhortation in this area is extremely rel-

evant today. Believers, today, have fallen into the same trap as the Church at Corinth, we are taking one another to court. Paul's message is clear; it is disgraceful for those who are walking in the light to go to those who are walking in darkness, to discern truth in a matter of dispute. Now certainly, there are some matters that have to be settled in court because of the laws that govern our land. However, whenever possible, the Church should mediate differences between Believers. Paul addresses the issue by discussing the rank, rule, righteousness, and riches of the redeemed.

1. **The Rank.** The rank of the redeemed ought to prevent us from feuding with one other in secular court. Paul says, "Dare any of you, having a matter against another go to law before the unjust, and not before the saints" (V.1)? Paul had to deal with a situation that was on-going and damaging to the testimony of the Church. Judgment ought to be handled between Believers by the Word of God and through the Church, not the court system. Believers have a special rank and responsibility because of our relationship with Jesus Christ. We will assist Christ in judging the world and angels (vv.2,3). This "judge factor" should help the Church discern truth in small matters that pertain to life. After all, we do have the mind of Christ. The Church should be embarrassed and ashamed for going to unbelievers for justice. Believers who refuse to settle their disputes through the Church, are usually motivated by greed or revenge.

2. **The Rule.** In addition to the rank of the redeemed, there is the rule of the redeemed, that should govern how we handle our differences. The rule is that there should be no fighting. Paul's exhortation to stay out of court for settling matters between two Believers is so strong that, we should be willing to suffer wrong

before going to court (1 Cor. 6:7). If we insist upon going to court to win the case, we have already lost spiritually. When we decide to strike back, Jesus is out of the equation. If we truly trust Jesus, we can allow ourselves to suffer wrong. It is His responsibility to avenge us, not ours.

3. **The Righteousness**. There should be no feud, no fight, and no filth. The righteousness of the redeemed ought to prevent us from taking each other to court. What we were before we were saved, and what we are after our salvation, ought to be as different as day and night. Christ *should* make a difference in the way we live.

4. **The Riches**. Finally, the riches of the redeemed ought to govern how we handle our differences. We have been washed and regenerated, even though we were at fault. We have a new point of conception. We have been sanctified, and set apart for the purposes of God. Not only have we been set apart, but we have been declared righteous (justified). Because of this, we should be lenient with Christians who are at fault with us.

Based upon our rank, the rule, our righteousness, and our riches, if we have a dispute with another believer it ought to be our Church, and not the courts, that help us settle our differences!

FREEDOM

Stand fast therefore in the liberty
wherewith Christ hath made us free,
and be not entangled again with
the yoke of bondage.

Galatians 5:1

Free From the Fractures of Life

Romans 8

One of the greatest assets of the born again Believer in Jesus Christ is the power of our freedom. In John 8, Jesus said, "If you continue in my Word, then you are my disciples and you will know the truth and the truth shall set you free." In Romans 8, the freedom Paul speaks of is an inner ability that protects us from being ambushed, prevents us from being alienated, and pre-empts us from the pollution and power of darkness. This freedom frees us to serve God; makes us free to be sanctified and satisfied in God. This freedom is unique, because it transfers us from the control of the flesh to the control of the spirit.

We as Believers are free in spite of the fears, fight, and friction of our everyday lives. In Romans 8, Paul deals with three areas regarding our freedom:

1. **Protection** (*We are Free from Destruction*). There is no condemnation, because we are totally saved on the merit of Jesus Christ. We are saved by Grace (love we do not deserve) through faith. Yet, it is necessary for Believers to continue in the war between the two natures, which will allows us to grow to be Christ-like. Knowing that there will be times when we will fall, fail, and fret. These are all part of growing up. As Believers, when we sin there are consequences, but there can never be condemnation. There are three things we need to remember as we battle the old nature:

    A. (Rom. 8:2) *The Law of Sin and Death cannot Claim Us.* Even though we still battle between the two natures, the old and the new, the law of sin and death cannot claim us because the law of Christ has made us free from it.

    B. (Rom. 8:3) *The Law of our Mind cannot Condemn Us.* The mind is weak through the flesh. The good news is, God sent Jesus who came in the "flesh" and overcame it. It is this Jesus who promises to helps us to overcome.

C. (Rom. 8:4) *The Law cannot Control Us.* When we are walking according to the law of Christ, He is on the inside, and He enables and empowers us through the Holy Spirit to walk right. We must yield to Christ. We are conditioned to sin, but God the Holy Spirit breaks the condition through the power of the Word.

2. **Prevention** *We are Free from Defeat.* Rom. 8:5-11, the unsaved don't have the Spirit of God, they live in and for the flesh; the unsaved are physically alive but spiritually dead. Christians have the Spirit, and they live in a different sphere of the Spirit. The unsaved cannot please God because they are too busy pleasing themselves.

3. **Preemption** *We are Free from Devastation.* Rom. 8:12-17. The Spirit gives us a desire to want to be like Jesus. He energizes us to walk and talk right. The Holy Sprit makes us want to pray, and cry out for help; thus devastation will not overtake us.

The fight is fixed. Everything that Satan throws at us will be used for God's Glory. Therefore, we have the victory. Though weeping may endure for a night, joy comes in the morning!

Aren't You Tired of Being a Slave?

All new products come with operating instructions. They provide the owner with the information necessary to empower them so that they get the optimum performance from the product. Galatians chapter 5 is a users manual for understanding the presence, power and priority of the Holy Spirit. Having already thoroughly established his argument for grace over works, Paul provides instructions on how to live the life of faith.

Paul begins with instruction on practical sanctification, as it relates to the freedom of the Believer. We must come to grips with the fact that the old nature only serves to keep us in bondage. On the other hand, the Holy Spirit's role is to be a helper, healer, and a habit breaker. Every Believer needs the Holy Spirit's ministry in their lives. We are all broken, bruised and battered by past experiences. Tragically, instead of experiencing the abundant life, the average Believer spends their lifetime coming up with strategies to protect themselves so that his brokenness is never revealed. In Galatians chapter 5, Paul describes three types of dysfunctional Believers: a slave, a debtor, and a runner.

1. **A Slave**: Paul begins Galatians chapter 5 with an exhortation to stand fast, therefore in the liberty wherewith Christ hath made us free. Though Christ has made us free, many believers still behave as slaves. We have been set free from a code of rules and from our sin nature. Christ has removed the chains, yet, we live like we are still in bondage. The truth is, Christ died and rose so that we would be set free; no longer slaves serving the old flesh nature. Not every slave wants to be released. The old nature counters the will, the way, and the Word of God. It will lie to us in order to perpetuate its rule over us. It must be rendered inoperative. We must learn to recognize when it is rising and make a decision to surrender to the Lordship of Jesus Christ, through the power of the Holy Spirit. We must choose to stand and walk in the liberty with which Christ has made us free (Gal. 5:1). When we fail to do so, we lose our liberty. Either we are slaves to sin or we are slaves for Christ.

2. **A Debtor**: Paul states, "For I testify again to every man that is circumcised, that he is a debtor to do the whole law" (Gal. 5:3). The slave looses his freedom, while the debtor loses his wealth. As Believers, we are not bankrupt. Instead, we have

been blessed with all spiritual blessings in heavenly places in Christ Jesus. When we function as debtors to the flesh, not only are we forfeiting the use of our wealth and wisdom, but we become frustrated and cause others to become fragmented. It is hypocritical to depend on the flesh. God wants us to come to Him broken. We are not to lean to our own understanding, but "in all our ways acknowledge Him and he shall direct our paths."

3. **A Runner**: The writer to the Hebrews, which I believe is the Apostle Paul, uses a metaphor of Running a Race (Heb. 12:1-5). This race is unique, because we are not running for salvation, but service. However, the word race, in the Hebrew, is agon (agony). Why is this "race" agonizing? Because it requires a persistence and a perserverence. This race is a marathon and not a sprint. The key is what we remove (weights or encumbrances), and rely on (faith) against the backdrop of the sin (unbelief) which easily besets (distracts) us. Finally, the race requires us to resist or to watch out for a wrong focus, "Looking unto Jesus the Author and Finisher of our faith..." (Heb. 12:2)

It is time to recoup our lost freedom, spiritual wealth and direction. We can experience the power, presence and priority of the Holy Spirit. We are not bound to the flesh nor do we have any obligation to serve it. Aren't you tired of being a slave? The Holy Spirit lives in us; He is our helper, healer and habit breaker!

A False Threat to the Church

Nearly everywhere we go, we find people troubled because they are insecure. They think that because of their sins, negligence, failing to endure to the end, or some other reason, they may lose their salvation. Those who believe that, although they are saved now, they are capable of losing their salvation later, have one of two problems. They are either trusting to some degree, in their works to save them or, they do not understand that by trusting Jesus Christ as Savior, their destiny is in God's hand.

People who believe that Salvation can be lost usually do not understand four things: 1) **Total Depravity**: there is nothing in fallen man that could commend him to God. 2) **Efficacious Grace**: Salvation is a free gift through faith, and is totally performed by God without help or cooperation. 3) **Sovereign and Eternal Election**: those who are saved have been chosen of God before the foundation of the world. 4) **Difference between Relationship** (John 3:16) **and Fellowship** (1 John 1:9).

All throughout the New Testament, God speaks of Eternal life (no beginning and no ending) and Everlasting life (a beginning but no ending). Sometimes these terms are interchangeable. People become confused because they really don't understand the *Plan of Salvation*. God uses a Payment Plan. His Payment Plan dictated that once the Payment was made in full (paid with the price that God requested), then Salvation would take place. The Bible's plan of salvation is this: Poor, unworthy sinners, who do not deserve anything good from God, can get forgiveness because Jesus paid for what we could never pay. He suffered what we ought to suffer, and God counted us righteous because of His Righteousness.

1. **God's Plan: The Credits of Christ's Payment Plan**: The *cost/payment* for our sin was the *death* of Christ, while the *provision* of the will is to *believe*. (Isaiah 53:4-6, II Corinthians 5:21, Romans 5:1, Romans 4:1-2).

2. **God's Position: The Character of Christ's Payment**: Since God promised payment, God must produce it. (Romans 5:8-11, Tutus 1-2, 1 John 2:25, 1 John 5:10-11, John 10:27-29, John 5:24, 1 Peter 1:3-5, John 6:39, Hebrews 10:9-10, and 7:25).

3. **God's Provision: The Conditions of Christ's Payment Plan**: The condition is that a person must be born again. Jesus says that a person who is born once, will die twice; once in the flesh and once in the Spirit. A twice-born person dies only once. He dies

in the flesh, but his soul lives forever. ***New Birth/Regeneration*** is the impartation of divine life to the Believer's soul. ***Impartation*** is what's divulged to you or for you (John 3:14-15, Numbers 21:4-9, John 3, John 3:16-18).

A Savior is one who takes you safely all the way to the shore. When God gives you eternal life, He will never cast you out or lose you. He means it. He is a true Savior.

Freedom from Bondage I

One of our greatest bondages has been our past. In a very real way, our past determines our future. The habits we've developed and the tastes we've cultivated have programmed our personalities, but the whole cluster of programmed responses was dealt with at the cross! We still feel the pull, and we find ourselves saying, "I can't help myself," or "this temptation is more than I can bear." We can yield to temptation, but we no longer have to.

Paul asked a rhetorical question, "Shall we continue to sin that grace may abound?" He said, "God forbid." In Romans 6, Paul is not talking about what kind of life the believer should live, but how they should live that life. He's not dealing with "sins" but "sin." Sin is singular, meaning, he is dealing with the old nature. In other words, shall we continue habitually to sustain the same relationship to the sinful nature that we sustained before we were saved? In chapter 6, we have the mechanics of the spirit-filled life. This machinery is what God sets up when He saves a person; the power of indwelling sin is broken, and the divine nature is implanted.

The Holy Spirit is the source of power and the operator of the spiritual machinery in the Believer. Self-dependence, when dropped into the inner workings of this machinery, stops the works, preventing the Holy Spirit from giving the Believer victory over the sinful nature. There are three indicators in a Believer's life, that prove there has been a surgical operation: (1) the death of the old man, (2) the death of the old methods, and (3) the death of the old master.

1. **First Indicator:** *Death of the Old Man*

    (a) <u>Spiritual Sending</u> (Gal.2:20, 5:24; Col. 33). We were placed in Christ by being baptized by the Holy Spirit. Furthermore, Christ places the Holy Spirit in us, which is the indwelling of the Holy Ghost.

    (b) <u>Spiritual Surgery</u> (Col.2:11, Heb.4:12). God cut the old nature from our souls to give us rest.

2. **Second Indicator:** *Death of the Old Methods*

    (a) Realizing that the power of the old nature was turned off, "*I can do all things through Christ*" (Phil. 4:3). The power being turned off, *frees* me to be able to do all things through Christ (Jn. 8:32-34).

(b) The position of the old nature has dropped (Eph.4:22; Col.3:5-9).

3. **Third Indicator:** *Death of the Old Master*

The new Master, Christ, changed those things I could not control (Jn.8:41-47; Col.2:12-15; Cor.15:25).

We need to recognize that we are dead to sin, reckon our decisions not to be controlled by sin, and righteously stand in the freedom wherewith Christ has made us free!

Freedom from Bondage II

With freedom, there is position of privilege, liberation from lock up, cancellation from custody, and release from another's requirement. Today, many Christians are enslaved to masters other than the Lord; we are chained to and crushed by behaviors that zap our blessings; we fight, but we are fractured; we pray, but we are pressured; we make resolutions, but still, we are restricted. Much of our dysfunction has nothing to do with Satan, but has to do with our unwillingness to change our lives and bring it under the control of the Holy Spirit. If we are to experience God's freedom of rest, relaxation, and righteous reward, we need to understand that there are some things from which we need to become free. Galatians 6:6-10 deals with freedom from bondage. In verse 7, Paul deals with our commitment to what we sow; we sow daily. Whatever we plant will spring up. God does not cut off the reaping process; it is the law of God. There are three freedoms we need:

1. **Freedom from Financial Debt.** The number one cause of the break up of marriages is money. We become enslaved and entrapped to creditors. There are three things concerning our financial freedom we must review. The first is how we govern our finances. We spend more than what is coming in. We must have a reasonable plan of action, so that we do not compromise our ethics before the Lord. The second is our problem with spending. We must differentiate between wants and needs. The third point has to do with how we give. God owns everything and He has given us things so that we can manage them. When we give the Lord His tithe, Malachi 3, says He will bless our ability to make money. If we are going to be free, we must be free in our finances.

2. **Freedom in Fellowship.** In Gal. 6:8, we are told to have character in how we sow. When we plant seeds that are fleshly and outside of the Spirit of God, it will lead to corruption. Paul teaches about the Fruit of the Spirit (which only the Spirit can produce). The list of the fruit (Gal. 5:22-23), can be divided into three areas: Love, Joy, and Peace, these are what every yielded Christian ought to have on the inside. Longsuffering, Gentleness, and Goodness are the outward expressions, which ought to be displayed toward others. The third group includes those things God ought to receive: Faith, Meekness (power under control), and Temperance (self-control). When we have a

righteous attitude, the result is peace, prosperity, and promotion. If we are to have freedom of fellowship, we are to have right attitudes, right actions, and right accountability.

3. **Fruitful Freedom**. In Gal. 6:9-10, we learn that there are some difficulties that come when we try to produce fruit. One of them is pain. This pain entails plowing up the land before we can plant, but we must not get weary when trying to do what is right. Why? There is a working principle; what we sow we will also reap (V.7). Yet, there is a process before we reap a harvest. The process includes pruning so that we can bear more fruit. The condition is that we faint not (V.9). If we faint, we will not see what Jesus has done in our lives. Therefore, we do not faint, lose faith, give up hope, get depressed, stop coming to church, stop participating in ministry, etc. If we are to have a fruitful freedom, we have to keep on moving.

A Functional Freedom

Relationships are directly connected to a particular function. When the function changes, our relationships change as well. A child who is very dependent upon his or her parents has established a dependent relationship, and the parents must pay close attention to the child. As the child matures, both the function and the relationship of both the parent and the child begin to change. These processes and changes are necessary for growth and maturity.

In Romans 7, God, through the Apostle Paul, is educating us on the proper relationship of the believer to the Law of Moses. This law has changed; we are no longer instructed to live out the law. When Jesus died, He died to deliver us from the law. The law was never meant to save us; it only bought defeat.

1. **The Premise of the Law in Relation to Believers** (Rom. 7:1-6). When Jesus died, since we were in Him, we died not only to sin, but also to the law. When He was buried and rose, so were we. Now that we are dead to sin and dead to the law, we are now free to marry Jesus. The law is not dead; we are dead to the law. Now we have a new partner, Christ, and we are able to bring forth fruit to God.

2. **The Purpose of the Law in Relation to Believers** (Rom. 7:7-13). The purpose of the law was to alert us and accuse us. Sin did not become sin until we heard the Word of God. Then the Holy Spirit worked inside us, and caused us to repent.

3. **The Problem of the Law in Relation to Believers** (Rom. 7:14-23). Paul reveals the defeat in the Law and his own carnality. The more we grow in Christ, the stronger we become, because we are learning how to live between the two natures.

4. **The Power over the Law in Relation to Believers** (Rom. 7:24-25). Paul acknowledged the wretched man that he was. Sin was a struggle for him, but he realized that only Jesus could free him from sin.

We now have a new function, because we have a new relationship. We have power and provision through Jesus. We have somebody who will handle our problems. God is making us strong so that when trouble comes in we can say, "I can do all things through Christ which strengthens me" (Phil. 4:13).

It Stands To Reason

Romans 8:31-39

One of the most important abilities God has given all human beings is the ability to reason. Unlike animals that are instinctive in nature, and react automatically to their surroundings in a particular manner, humans are different. Humans were made in the image of God. We have an intellect, volition, will and emotions. We were created as moral creatures. God has given humans the ability to rationalize, reason, and respond after analyzing a situation. We are able to see purpose, process, procedure, meaning, method, objective, and outcome.

In Rom. 8:31-39, Paul reminds us that there is no condemnation to those that are in Christ. We are free from destruction because of the righteousness of Jesus Christ. We are free from defeat because of the power of the indwelling Holy Spirit, who enables us to overcome the sin nature. There is no discouragement because of the hope that is in us. There is also no division from the love of God, because there is no separation from Christ. Paul begins an argument with four rhetorical questions which need no answer, if we really know the character of God.

1. **By Reason of God's Power** (Rom. 8:31-32). *If God be for us who can be against us?* Paul has established that circumstances cannot hurt us. The Holy Spirit is causing our circumstances to work out for our good and for His Glory.

   Although Satan appears to be strong, having some power, Jesus has all power. We need to know that God is on our side. Since God gave us His best, His Son (Jesus), will He not give us the rest?

2. **By Reason of God's Position** (Rom. 8:33). *Who shall lay anything to the charge of God's elect?* In other words, who shall accuse us? It is the goodness of God that leads us to repentance, through the conviction of the Holy Spirit. On the other hand, Satan is an accuser of the brethren. We must understand the difference between guilt (Satan), and conviction (Holy Spirit). Remember, God has not dealt with us according to our sins, nor has He rewarded us according to our iniquities.

3. **By Reason of God's Priesthood** (Rom. 8:34). *Who is he that condemneth?*

Jesus died, was buried, rose, and ascended at the right hand of the Father, so that when we believe, there is no condemnation. Additionally, the Holy Spirit helps us to live right. He restores us every time we want to give up and go back to our old ways.

4. **By Reason of God's Protection** (Rom. 8:35-39). *Who can separate us from the love of Christ?* Death, to the Believer, is a door to deliverance. It does not separate us from His love. Circumstances will not last for the Believer, and it will not separate us from His love. Nothing can prevent God from loving us; not Satan, sin, or self. Nothing can stand between the believer and Jesus Christ.

What kind of love is this? This love is "Agape" love; a love we will never deserve.

Freedom is not just having the liberty to do as one pleases. Rather, it is an enablement in which one is able to participate in and serve another's purpose. Freedom is the ability to have peace, power, and put away personal prerogatives.  True freedom evidences itself in not running, but remaining; not in fainting, but being faithful; in being diligent in our delays and purposeful in our problems. Freedom frees us from entanglements and entrapments. When we attain freedom, we are free from unbiblical beliefs, unbiblical behavior, and from a sense of being bothered. The more freedom we experience, the less things bother us because we know Who is in control. Once we understand the freedom we have in Jesus, we start trusting and entrusting things to Him, knowing that He will work it out. In 2 Corinthians, Paul outlines what true Biblical freedom involves.

1. **Freedom Allows Us to Stand**. In 2 Cor. 11, Paul tells the church that we must stand. We cannot be free if we are afraid to stand. There are two things we must stand against. The first is, *error* (V.3). We must have a fearlessness to confront error, and stand against that which is false. Secondly, we must stand against *enemies*. In Corinth, false apostles came into the church from the outside to oppose Christians (V.4). When we take a stand for what is right, we must expect opposition.

2. **Freedom Allows Us to Submit**. There are three things we need to do in order to submit. First, we must give up personal power. Paul speaks of laying aside his personal power by not charging the church wages for preaching the gospel (vv.7-8). Secondly, we must lay aside our personal position (V.9). Paul speaks of humbling himself to exalt Christ (vv.7-19). Third, we must lay aside our prerogatives. Jesus came in the form of a servant, even though, God the Father and God the Son are equal. As Isaac allowed Abraham to tie him down, Jesus allowed the Father to put Him on the cross. Jesus submitted to the Father. He laid aside His prerogatives. Submission is based on knowledge. In John 13, Jesus knew the Father had put all power into His hands, yet, He washed the disciples' feet. If we know we are in Christ, that Jesus is our power base, and that we have all things in Him, then we are able to serve others. Submission allows us to serve one another, it allows us to help one another, and it allows us to be there for one another without worrying about what others will do for us.

3. **Freedom Allows Us to Suffer**. We need freedom to suffer so that we can graciously glorify God. Paul speaks of his sufferings for Christ (vv.22-26). He was beaten, stoned, shipwrecked, and put in peril and danger. Paul suffered in personal crises: "in labor and hardship, through many sleepless nights, in hunger and thirst, often without food, in cold and exposure" (vv.27-29). Paul suffered in confidence; he gloried in his infirmities (V.30). Freedom is being able to see suffering from God's perspective. Freedom is being able to sing His praises in the midst of problems, for He is too wise to make a mistake.

We must be free to stand against error and the enemies of the cross. Free to submit in our time of crisis, and free to suffer for the Name of Jesus.

PEACE

And the very God of peace sanctify you
wholly; and I pray God your whole spirit
and soul and body be preserved blameless
unto the coming of our Lord Jesus Christ.

1 Thessalonians 5:23

Be Still in the Storm

One of the greatest challenges faced by Believers is the act of being still in the midst of the storm, to pause in the midst of our problems, and to remain calm in the center of our confusion. In Nehemiah chapter 5, the Jews that had returned from Babylonian captivity had a desire to rebuild. However, they were faced with major roadblocks. In Neh. 2, they were discouraged, in Neh. 3 they were displaced. In Ch. 4, they were disillusioned. In Neh. 5, they were faced with delay, difficulty, depression, and devastation. Nehemiah is cautioned to comfort the people because of an unusual attack. As Believers, we must be aware that Satan has a strategy, and his deeds are deadly:

1) He deceives us with false security,
2) He discourages us by putting our feelings against our faith,
3) He destroys our relationships by attacking our emotions,
4) He divides our purposes,
5) He creates doubts in our prayers,
6) He devastates the program that God has for us,
7) He deepens our sense of hurt by putting our attention on our strongholds.

On the other hand, God allows delays, difficulty and devastation to help develop us and deepen our walk with Him. The Lord gives us discernment about where He wants us to go. In Neh. 5, Satan changes the strategy. The attack is no longer from the external enemies, it is now internal attacks. Internal attacks are much deeper than the outward attacks. It is in this context of delayed difficulty and devastation that the brethren became bothered and families became fragmented.

Nehemiah must go into deep prayer to receive God's strategy. The people were preoccupied with the walls. They had left the raising of the crops to go to the raising of the walls. This attack is internal. There will be times when we will wonder why the storm, with the winds and the rain.

1. **A Loving Counsel** (Neh. 5:7-10). We need a reverence for Jesus. We need to spend time alone with the Savior to seek His face, and to reverentially trust (fear) Him. We need to submit to His sovereignty, knowing He can and will do what He wants to do in our lives. God knows what we are going through, and

He had already ordered our deliverance before we entered into our difficulty.

2. **A Communion with God** (Neh. 5:10). When trouble comes, and we cannot pray, the Holy Spirit is right there with us. He takes every "moan" back to God, because He knows what we need.

3. **A Liberated Calm** (Neh. 5:14). We experience a calmness, when we are trusting God in the presence of external enemies, and there are wounds on the inside. We have no control over these things. We need God right now. Psalm 107 advises that we need to believe God is good, regardless of what we are going through; "The Lord is good and His mercy endureth forever."

"Oh, that men would praise the Lord." In our delays, difficulties, and devastation, God gives us clarity, communion, and a calmness.

God's Rule for Rest

Of all the rules found in the Word of God that govern the life of the believer, there is one rule that we tend to neglect in our attempt to become free. That is the rule of God's peace. Throughout Paul's epistle to the Colossians, he uses a key word, the word "*let*." The word *let* implies that we must give God the control. There are two "lets" in Col. 3:15-16: "Let the peace of God rule in your heart *and* Let the Word of God dwell in you richly in all wisdom." In order to let the peace of God rule in our hearts, we must let the Holy Spirit be the umpire. The Holy Spirit is the One who will cause us to stand in the midst of storms.

Paul points out two aspects of peace: 1) peace with God (Rom. 5:1), which gives us our salvation, and 2) the peace of God (Phil. 4:7), which gives us our rest. We have peace with God for eternity (eternal security), and we have the peace of God when we are in the will of God (conditional promise). As long as David was covering up his sin, he had no peace. He had to confess his sin, trust God for his forgiveness, and do the will of God before peace was restored, then he could praise God. We must let the peace of God protect us from three enemies:

1. **Worry**. The first enemy of the Believer is worry (Phil. 4:6). A lack of faith not only causes us to worry, but also causes us to fear and fret. Phil. 4:6 gives us a formula for not falling prey to worry. We are to pray (worship), petition, and then praise Him through thanksgiving. Then "the peace of God that passes all understanding will keep (the word "keep" means "to guard"), our hearts and minds" (V.7). When we pray according to His will, God erases our worrying.

2. **Wounds**. We have all been wounded in some way. In Luke 10:30, Jesus explains the parable of the Good Samaritan. There was a certain man going to Jericho from Jerusalem. The journey was treacherous. The man was wounded by thieves and left for dead. After the religious men passed him, a Samaritan came by and had compassion for him. The Samaritan "lived out" his compassion by putting oil on the man's wounds. Compassion is an action. The Samaritan then took the wounded man to an inn and paid for two days worth of care. The mission of the church is not only to have compassion, but also to meet people where they are, help heal the wounds, bring joy through healing, and

to support spiritually, those who cannot support themselves. The Holy Spirit wants to be our umpire over our wounds.

3. **Warfare.** Our objective is to remain standing after Satan has hit us with everything (Eph. 6:10-11). Thus, we need the whole armor of God. The strategy of Satan is first, to bring on distrust in God's goodness and character. Second, he wants us to become disobedient to God's Word. Therefore, our circumstances should never lead us to compromise the Word. The shield, which is our doctrinal integrity, will hold off the darts of the enemy. The helmet of salvation protects our mind. In addition, the sword, which is the Word, will help us fight back.

Therefore, let us stand firm by letting the peace of God keep our hearts and minds through Christ Jesus and by letting the Holy Spirit be our umpire.

Peace In spite of Our Pitfalls

II Corinthians - Chapter 5

One of our resources for rest and rejuvenation is the truth, the triumph, and the transforming power of the Word of God. God's Word strengthens us and soothes our souls in times of trouble. When we are ready to give up, God sends a fitted Word to keep us going. Paul, the Apostle, reminds us that, although, we have had trials, now we have triumph. Too often we look to the world for motivation, when we really need to look to Christ. God is doing good things in our lives, not because we desire or deserve it, but because we are a child of the King. He promised that He would work out our good and His Glory. Rom. 8:28, "And we know that all things work together for good to them that love God, to them who are the called according to His purpose".

1. **Our Confidence in Death** (2 Cor. 5:1). Death to the unbeliever is doom. When the unbeliever dies, they go to hell with the conscientiousness that they could have accepted the Lord Jesus Christ as Savior (Luke 15). If we are saved, then, when our earthly bodies dissolve, God has a building not made by hands; He has prepared a mansion for our glorified bodies. The moment we as Believers die, we are in the presence of Jesus. Those already in heaven would not want to come back because being with Jesus is more beautiful than life on earth.

2. **Our Conflict in Difficulty** (2 Cor. 5:2-8). It is because we are in the flesh, that we groan for deliverance. We want to please God through doing what's right, but our flesh keeps pulling us back into sin. God allows conflict to interfere with our calling. We must experience friction to fully realize God's will for our lives. God allows conflict so that we will desire to be with Him.

3. **Our Comfort in Delay** (2 Cor. 5:9-16). Our aim should be to please Christ and to be in the place where He desires for us. It is the goodness of God that leads men to repentance. What have we done in Jesus' Name? Have we been faithful to the Word? Have we prayed and led others to Christ? What will we have to lay before Jesus' feet? We all will appear before the Judgment seat of Christ. Are we in a state of delay due to our disobedience or disagreement?

4. **Our Confirmation in Deliverance** (2 Cor. 5:17-21). We are a new creation in Christ. When Christ comes in, He sets up new things: acceptance, assurance, armor, and a Christ-like divine nature. Old things are passed away; value systems, old priorities, old beliefs, old plans, and old masters who had control over our lives. We are new today. We may not feel like it, but it is not about our feelings, it is all about our faith in the finished work of the Lord Jesus Christ.

We go to church because the Holy Spirit pricks our hearts to worship Him for Who He is. We are ambassadors for Christ. We should be witnessing about Jesus on our jobs and in our communities. We all make mistakes, but God, who is rich in mercy (Eph. 2:4). God will teach us how to make things right and give us strength and power to endure our failures. Let's trust God in our self-made turmoil, and thank Him for His Perfect Person, Plan, Perspective and Peace (the Lord Jesus Christ), in the midst of our Pitfalls.

PROMISES
(WITH CONDITIONS)

He staggered not at the promise of God
through unbelief; but was strong in faith,
giving glory to God;

Romans 4:20

Protected By a Promise

One of the greatest vehicles of God's vision is His use of the past to preview the future. He uses a *story* to explain a strategy, a *type* to emphasize a truth, and a *people* to usher in a Person who has a program. The Bible is an organized, gradual unfolding of God's plan of redemption. The Pentateuch, specifically deals with the ministry, the movement, and the mandate for the nation of Israel. It contains the purpose, the principles, and the placement of the nation. In Exodus 19 and 20, Israel arrives in the wilderness of Sinai. They had passed through the Red Sea (Ex.14), they had heard the song of Miriam (Ex.15), they had received manna from heaven (Ex.16), and they had received water from a rock (Ex.17). It is in the context of Ex. 19, that God speaks to Moses at Sinai. God says, "I bore you on Eagle's wings and I brought you to Myself" (Ex. 19:4). An Eagle has five qualities that can be observed in order to learn about God:

1. **God Cares for Us**. The eagle cares for its eaglets by feeding and nurturing them. Similarly, God cared for His people by redeeming them out of bondage, through the blood of the Passover lamb. God also cares for the Church. He has redeemed us out of spiritual bondage, through the blood of Jesus.

2. **God Carries Us**. The eagle removes her eaglets to protect them. The Lord has removed us from the world just as He moved the Israelites out of danger. Because of the Lord's deliverance, they were not to lust after that which they left in Egypt. Neither are we to look back to the days before our salvation.

3. **God Counsels Us**. The eagle counsels the eaglets by teaching them how to fly. Sometimes God counsels us through correction (Heb. 12:6). God rebuked Israel at Kadesh Barnea and kept them in the wilderness for forty years. The mother eagle teaches the eaglet how to fly by dropping it from a lofty place. When the eaglet looks like it will not make it, the mother eagle catches it, and then drops it again. Likewise, God is teaching us how to walk in the light and how to overcome sin. We do not learn how to fly (walk the Christian life), until we are dropped. God allows some things in our lives just to help us to fly.

4. **God Compels Us**. Soon the eaglets are old enough to make their own nests and to hunt for themselves. As God renews us, He compels us to start our own spiritual nests. We have

the Holy Spirit who prays for, pardons and promotes us in the Name of Jesus. That is why Isaiah said, "Have you not known? Have you not heard? The everlasting God, the LORD, the Creator of the ends of the earth neither faints nor is He weary. His understanding is unsearchable. He gives power to the weak" (Isaiah 40:28-29). The Holy Spirit gives us power when we are ready to give up. He mends, motivates, moves, and manages us. Isaiah goes on to say that, even the youth get weary and fall. "But they that wait on the LORD shall renew their strength. They will mount up with wings like eagles; they will run and not get weary; they will walk and not faint" (Isaiah 40:31). When God's strength becomes our strength, then we are strong for the journey. When we get tired and weary we must do as Isaiah says, "They that wait upon the LORD shall renew their strength."

5. **God Cautions Us**. He made the Israelites thirst, brought hard times, and tested them so they would remember that it was not by might, but by His Spirit.

We must, also, remember from whence we came. We must remember that Jesus bore us on eagle's wings by redeeming us, removing us, rebuking us, renewing us, and restoring us. He is worthy to be praised because He bore us on eagle's wings.

The Cycle of Life

Ephesians 2:1 & 3:19

The histories of great civilizations can remind us of a giant revolving door. It turns on the axis of human depravity as its movement is marked by the perimeter of time. With monotonous repetition, each civilization has completed the same cycle, having passed through a similar sequence of events. It could look like this:

1. *From bondage to spiritual faith*
2. *From spiritual faith to great courage*
3. *From courage to strength*
4. *From strength to abundance*
5. *From abundance to leisure*
6. *From leisure to selfishness*
7. *From selfishness to complacency*
8. *From complacency to apathy*
9. *From apathy to dependency*
10. *From dependency to weakness*
11. *From weakness back to bondage*

Thus, life appears to be a cycle. From this perspective, Israel can teach us a lesson through the window of the book of "Judges." Israel had a movement that turned into a cycle of over 300 years. The Israelites lived in bondage; God gave them a deliverer, liberty, abundance, leisure, and they ended up, back in bondage. The age-old revolving door is turning, and we are somewhere between apathy and dependency. A revolving door has to be pushed by those within it; only when we stop pushing, will it stop turning, but not a moment before. Much the same way, every Christian must make a push to obey the new nature in him, so that the sinful nature will not exercise *lordship* over us. Paul even gives the reason why when he says, "You are not under law, but under grace." To be under law refers to an unsaved person who attempts to live in obedience to the law of God. To be under grace refers to the saved person who has been the subject of a surgical operation, where the power of the sinful nature has been broken and divine power implanted.

Paul tells us to stop allowing the sinful nature to reign as king. We must stop putting our members at the disposal of the sinful nature. For we as Christians, have been given the power and ability to yield to the new nature. Grace is not lenient; it is far stricter than the law. The Holy Spirit, who indwells the Believer, takes notice of the slightest sin and convicts him of it. Whereas, the law can act only generally, and then only when the conscience of the individual cooperates with it. The deterrent to sin is the power of divine love (Gal.5:13).

1. **Favor**. Paul brings out three benefits the Believer receives by yielding to the new nature. It is because of God's grace that we yield ourselves to Him and we receive His *Favor* (Ex.11:3; Prov.8:35, 14:9, and Dan.1:9).

2. **Freedom**. The unsaved person is free from righteousness, but his bondage to sin only leads him deeper into slavery, so that it becomes harder and harder to do right. While the prodigal son was at home, he decided that he wanted his freedom, so he left home to enjoy himself. However, his rebellion led him into deeper slavery. He was the slave of wrong desires and wrong deeds. As he yielded to his father, he found true freedom.

3. **Fruit**. If we serve a master, we expect to receive wages. Sin pays wages; death. God also pays wages; holiness and everlasting life. Let us not fulfill the lusts of the flesh, but display the fruit of the Spirit, as we walk in the light as He is the light.

Samson, in Judges 16, yielded himself to the lusts of the flesh and the result was death. If the believer refuses to surrender his body, he is in danger of the Father's discipline. But the gift of God, in spite of all of our sins, is eternal life. Paul said, "...thanks be to God for His unspeakable gift..." What a gift and what a Giver!

Do You Know What's Behind You?

Experiencing the precious promises of God is the greatest privilege of the Believer. There is a plethora of promises available to us. These promises include: provision, protection, promotion, pre-emption, and power. God provides these promises as a covering in the midst of our chaos. We have the assurance that when we are in trouble these promises are in place. Nothing can alter or interfere with the promises of God. Yet, some are conditional; access is based upon our belief, behavior, and our ability  to be still. While others are unconditional, and continue to surround us, in spite of our disobedience and doubt.

1. **The Purpose of Promises**: In general, promises have purpose. God uses them for our development and direction. The development addresses our needs. "He who has begun a good work in you will perform it until the day of Jesus Christ" (Phil. 1:6). We also get direction, "I will instruct you, teach and guide you in the way you should go"(Ps. 32:8). Promises give power and protection, "No weapon formed against you shall prosper" (Is. 54:17). Additionally, they supply peace, pre-empt trouble, and promote our good.

2. **A Place of Promises**: Psalm 23, one of the most quoted Psalms, is filled with promises. Though many can quote the passage, only a very few can qualify its promises. This psalm teaches us that the Lord leads, feeds and liberates. In it we find purpose, power, provision, protection, peace and passion.

   A. **Purpose**: "The Lord is my Shepherd I shall not want". As my Shepherd, the Lord is my Manager and Director. I come under His control. Making the Lord our personal manager indicates we have surrendered our wills. It is His agenda and priorities that we carry out. *The salvation experience does not automatically make the Lord our Shepherd.* God the Father is the Author of creation; God the Son is the Artist of creation, and God the Holy Spirit is the Agent by which Jesus Christ comes and is revealed in the life of the Believer. With these priorities in place, we will not lack anything, and understand our purpose for living; bringing glory to the Lord Jesus Christ.

   B. **Peace**: "He maketh me to lie down in green pastures". He makes us rest. Sheep won't lie down if there is fear, friction, flies, or fretting, because they are not being fed. Like sheep, we need His direction. We also enjoy the Shepherd's presence, provisions, and green pastures. "He leadeth me beside the still waters." Sheep require a lot of water to avoid dehydration, and the water must come from a still, non-polluted source. Otherwise, thirst will cause sheep to get restless. Only Jesus can satisfy our thirst; He is the Living Water.

C. **Protection**: "He restoreth my soul." His restoration process is quiet and effective. Fear and frustration cause us to panic. The shepherd must come and get us back on our feet. "He leadeth me in the path of righteousness for His Name's sake". Sheep are creatures of habit. They graze in the same place. The Shepherd has a plan to lead us, like sheep, into new arenas of truth, to keep us healthy and strong.

D. **Presence**: "Yea, though I walk through the valley of the shadow of death, I will fear no evil: for thou art with me." The Shepherd takes his sheep to high country. Sheep are secure and content with the Shepherd. There are some valleys they must go through on their journey together, but the Shepherd sticks close to the sheep. "Thy rod and thy staff they comfort me." The rod represents the Word which disciples, disciplines and delivers us. The Staff represents the Spirit of God who is our Comforter. A shepherd uses the staff to guide, comfort and keep the sheep together.

5. **Provision**: Thou preparest a table in presence of my enemies." This table is choice grass. "Thou anointest my head with oil." Nose flies aggravate sheep, so the shepherd applies the oil to eliminate the irritation. The oil brings immediate rest. "My cup runneth over." Blessings are innumerable in the company of the shepherd. "Surely goodness and mercy shall follow me all the days of my life: and I will dwell in the house of the Lord for ever." We have assurance of His grace throughout our lives.

Psalm 23 is filled with the promises of His Presence in our lives. Whenever, we feel the need for reassurance, we can look to Psalm 23 to calm and to comfort us in the knowledge of the Lord Jesus Christ.

242

A Misunderstanding of God's Contract

Whenever there is an agreement, whether it is a covenant or a contract, there are certain clauses or stipulations that must be understood. There are both clauses and coverage which specify the extent of the coverage, as well as who is covered. We may have full coverage, but if we do not understand our agreement and the stipulations of the contract, we become confused. People in the Church have wrong concepts of God's contract; they think they can be hearers, but not doers. People in the world think they can sow  without reaping. What they do not understand is that God's Word is a *contract* with different stipulations. One of the major reasons for confusion, bewilderment, and fear is because God's *contract* to man has been misread, misinterpreted, and misrepresented. God's contract for the Church has three clauses:

1. **Insurance** (Family Clause): Belonging insures us of salvation and is based on an *unconditional* relationship. We are insured against Hell, and against self, and against sin. There is only one deductible, and that is Belief (John 3:16, 5:24, 6:28-30). This Family Clause has nothing to do with work, church, baptism, or even obedience. The sin from which we have been delivered from has three departments:

    A. The Penalty of Sin (Past): We have been delivered.
    B. The Power of Sin (Present): We are being delivered.
    C. The Presence of Sin (Future): We will be delivered.

The Family Clause includes:

    A. Regeneration: A new Life from God.
    B. Conversion: A new Attitude toward God.
    C. Justification: A new State before God.
    D. Redemption: A new Purchase of God.

2. **Assurance** (Finality Clause): Behavior assures us that we will never lose communion or fellowship with our Insurer. We are set apart by His sanctifying work (1 John 2:3-4, 4:17-18, 3:7-10).

3. **Issuance** (Followship Clause): God says our blessings are predicated on our fellowship and our obedience to His Word (John 15:7). There are some byproducts of fellowship and "follow-ship." One of these blessings is rest:

    A. Rest for the Sinner (Matthew 11:28) *At the Cross*
    B. Rest for the Saint (Matthew 11:29) *In Subjection*
    C. Rest in the Lord (Ps. 36:7) *In Confidence*
    D. Rest in the Lord (II Thes. 1:7) *In Glory*
    E. Rest that Remains (Hebrews 4:9) *Eternal*

When we get into trouble, all we have to do is look at God's Contract, Clauses, and Stipulations. That Contract reveals God's Promises.

RESURRECTION

Jesus said unto her, I am the
resurrection, and the life: he that
believeth in me, though he were dead,
yet shall he live:
John 11:25

An Open and Shut Case

The resurrection of the **Lord Jesus Christ** was a mysterious mission of mercy, as the Son of God rose from the dead in order to redeem mankind. Just three days earlier the crowds were confused; how could the Master be muffled; how could the Savior be silenced; how could the Lord be lynched? Additionally, the sky had darkened, the earth started rocking and reeling, and graves were opened. These occurances affected people in different ways. The disciples were disappointed, the women were emotionally wounded, and the Sadducees were satisfied. Jesus, the proclaimed prophet, was dead. How could someone with the power to feed five thousand with only a small substance of food, raise the dead, and turn water into wine, allow the Romans and the Jews to put Him up on the cross, rendering Himself helpless?

Jesus is depicted differently in each book of the Gospels. The book of Matthew depicts Jesus as the *Messiah*. The book of Mark depicts Him as the *Miracle Worker*. The book of John depicts Him as *Divine Maker*. But the book of Luke depicts Him *as Mediator*. Luke tells us that He had to be one hundred percent God and one hundred percent man. It is in this backdrop of His perfect manhood, that Luke begins to reveal the Christ.

In Luke 24, Mary Magdalene, Johanna, Mary the mother of James and other women, ran to the grave early. Angels met them at an empty tomb, asking, "why they were looking for the living amongst the dead." Following the incident at the empty tomb, two disciples, on the way to Emmaus, were troubled and perplexed; their Messiah was gone. Finally, Jesus revealed Himself to them. Jesus then, "opened their understanding, that they might understand scriptures" (Luke 24:45).

The disciples were disoriented because they did not understand the plan, purpose, place, payment, nor the power of God. They did not understand God's divine vision of redemption, which included the resurrection.

He got up with nail prints still in His hands and feet, and a hole in His side, but He walked out of the tomb early Sunday morning. The Resurrection proved to mankind five major components of God's all-wise counsel.

1. The Resurrection Fulfilled God's Plan.

2. The Resurrection Foretold His Purpose.

3. The Resurrection Fixed God's place in His Prophecy.

4. The Resurrection Finalized God's Payment.

5. The Resurrection was a Function of God's Power.

Jesus is throughout the alphabet: Almighty, Alpha, Beginning, Comforter, Deliver, Everlasting Father, Faithful, Governor, Glory, Head of the Church, High Priest, Holy one of God, I Am, Jesus, Judge, Justifier, King, Lamb, Lord, Master, Mediator, Mighty God, Nazarene, Omnipotent, Passover, Prince, Prophet, Power, Priest, Rabbi, Ransom, Redeemer, Righteousness, Savior, Seed, Shepherd, Son of God, Son of Man, Teacher, Wonderful, The Word, He is King of kings, Lord of lords. He is Alpha and Omega, and everything in between.

His Resurrection Was a Must

I Corinthians 15:25

There was an eerie hush over the city of Jerusalem, a hush that evidenced a brutal week of hatred. Sunday, a week prior, Jesus ride triumphantly from Bethany through Jerusalem. It marked the official presentation of the King. On Monday, Jesus cursed the fig tree, symbolizing the curse of the nation of Israel, and then the cleansing of the temple. Tuesday, witnesses watchd the fig tree wither and heard parables explained; Mary anoints the Messiah, and Judas plots the betrayal. Thursday, witnesses a preparation for the Passover, the disciples' feet are washed, Judas is revealed and defects, and Jesus experiences the grief at Gethsemane. Friday, the betrayal takes place. Jesus is arrested and brought before Annanias, the High Priest, who then transfers Him in order to be interrogated. Peter denies Jesus three times. Jesus is condemned. Judas commits suicide. Jesus is transferred to Herod, then retransferred to Pilate, marched by Roman soldiers, and led to Golgotha to be tormented on the cross. He dies and is buried 6pm on Friday.

Dead and gone, everyone is baffled, bewildered, and confused as to whether they would ever see Him again. But as, the Apostle Paul, informs us, He had to rise again. Every incident that happened during the course of that terrible week had been prophesied and typically displayed in the Old Testament. There are many reasons why He arose from the dead.

1. He had to rise because all **Prophesies Pointed to Him** (I Cor. 15:3, 4).

    A. *His Triumphal Entry* (Zech. 9:9). "Rejoice greatly O daughter of Zion! Shout, O daughter of Jerusalem! Behold your King is coming to you. He is just and having salvation, lowly and riding on a donkey, a colt, the foal of a donkey.

    B. *Unbelief* (Isa. 53:1). "Who has believed our report, and to whom has the arm of the Lord been revealed?"

    C. *Betrayed By a Close Friend* (Ps. 41:9). "Even my own familiar friend in whom I trusted, who ate my bread, has lifted up his heel against me."

    D. *Spat On and Struck* (Isa. 50:6). "I gave my back to those who struck me and my cheeks to those who plucked out the beard. I did not hide my face from shame and spitting."

E. *Vicarious Sacrifice* (Isa. 53:5). "He was wounded for our transgressions. He was bruised for our iniquities: the chastisement of our peace was upon Him, and with His stripes we are healed."

F. *No Broken Bones* (Isa. 34:20). "He guards all His bones, not one of them is broken."

G. *To Be Resurrected* (Psa. 16:10). "For you will not leave my soul in Sheol, nor will you allow your Holy One to see corruption."

H. *To Redeem* (Psalms 43:15), "But God will redeem my soul from the power of the grave. For He shall receive me. Selah."

2. He had to rise because all Old Testament **Prisoners waited for Him** (I Cor. 15:12-19, Luke 16:19). Jesus led a triumphal procession into Glory. The lost are still there. We know this estate changed, because when Stephen in Acts was stoned, he went up into glory and sees Jesus standing in Heaven. Paul said, "to be absent from the body is to be present with the Lord."

3. He had to rise because all of **God's Programs Needed Him** (I Cor. 15:21-28). The Church, the Millennium, and the Eternal State.

Night of the Living Dead

The greatest remedy for the people of God is to be rescued, redeemed, and restored by our Lord and Savior Jesus Christ. God's restoration is much more than resuscitation. It's a renewal that leads to a richness of fellowship and followship. When God resurrects, He allows the old to completely die and then renews life through a process called regeneration. If there were any question as to who holds the dead and who has power over hell, the answer can be found in Ezekiel 37. This is where resurrection is realized, complication is minimized, inspiration is prophesized, and restoration is mobilized. It is only here that we will see dead men walk and ghosts talk. Only Jesus can do these things. Chapters 36 and 37 lay out a rich restoration of Israel from the grave to God's Glory. Ezekiel lays out God's three-fold operation.

1. **God's Strange Inquiry** (The Challenge - Ez. 37:1-5). There was a motivation. God starts to educate the prophet. He has Ezekiel observe some dry bones. God asks, "Can these dry bones live?" (V.3) Many times in our lives, God will carry us into troubled areas and ask us some questions, when He already knows the answer. God may ask, "Can the bones of your issues be resolved, the bones of your unbelief, and lack of spirituality?" Can they come back to life again?

2. **God's Strategic Initiative** (The Channel - Ez. 37:6-10). There was a message. God told Ezekiel to preach to the dry bones. Ezekiel heard from God and a regeneration process started. God gave him a promise that the bones would come back to life, and it took both the Word and the Spirit. Regeneration and resurrection will lead to restoration.

3. **God's Supernatural Intention** (The Change - Ez. 37:11-28). God explains to Ezekiel that the dry bones are Israels; dead because of their captivity in Babylon. However, God would give those dry bones life, and He would restore them to the land of Israel again. This would be done by God's Spirit (Ez. 37:14). Through the Work of the Holy Spirit, God brings back together what we have torn apart. He helps our displacements, so that we are not out of place anymore. Most of us are where God wants us to be, because God specializes in resurrection, regeneration, and restoration.

Jesus is the Resurrection and the Light. God asked, "son of man, can these bones live?" We may have broken, bruised, and battered bones, but He is able to resurrect and restore. That is what makes Him God. He will give us life when we are dead and give us hope when we are hopeless. Dead bones can get up, alcoholics can sober up, drug addicts can stop doing drugs, weary children can come home, bodies can be healed, and problems can be turned into praise, in the Name of Jesus!